The Fast-Track MBA Series

Co-published with AMED (the Association for Management Education and Development)

Consultant Editors
John Kind, Director, Harbridge Consulting Group
David Megginson, Associate Head, Sheffield Business School

THE FAST-TRACK MBA SERIES represents an innovative and refreshingly different approach to presenting core subjects in a typical MBA syllabus in a lively and accessible way. The usual text book approach is eschewed in favour of a practical, action-oriented style which involves the reader in self-assessment and participation.

Ideal for managers wanting to renew or develop their management capabilities, the books in *THE FAST-TRACK MBA SERIES* rapidly give readers a sound knowledge of all aspects of business and management that will boost both self-confidence and career prospects. For those fortunate enough to take an MBA, the *Series* will provide a solid grounding in the subjects to be studied. Managers and students worldwide will find this new series an exciting and challenging alternative to the usual study texts and management guides.

Titles already available in the series are:

★ *Strategic Management* (Robert Grant & James Craig)
★ *Organisational Behaviour and Design* (Barry Cushway & Derek Lodge)
★ *Problem Solving and Decision Making* (Graham Wilson)
★ *Human Resource Development* (David Megginson, Jennifer Joy-Matthews & Paul Banfield)
★ *Accounting for Managers* (Graham Mott)
★ *Human Resource Management* (Barry Cushway)
★ *Macroeconomics* (Keith Wade and Francis Breedon)
★ *Employability* (Susan Bloch and Terry Bates)

Forthcoming books in the series will cover:

Data Analysis and IT ★ Financial Management ★ International Management ★ Investment and Risk ★ Law ★ Business Ethics ★ Marketing ★ Operations Management.

AMED is an association of individuals who have a professional interest in the development of people at work. AMED's network brings together people from industry, the public sector, academic organizations and consultancy, and is exclusive to individuals.

The aims of AMED are to promote best practice in the fields of individual and organizational development, to provide a forum for the exploration of new ideas, to offer members opportunities for their own development and to encourage the adoption of ethical practices in development.

For further information on AMED you are invited to write to AMED, 14–15 Belgrave Square, London SW

D1469001

The Series Editors

John Kind is a director of Harbridge House, a consultancy firm specializing in management development and training. He has wide experience of designing and presenting business education programmes in various parts of the world for clients such as BAA, Bass, British Petroleum and General Electric. John Kind is a visiting lecturer at Henley Management College and holds an MBA from the Manchester Business School and an honours degree in Economics.

David Megginson is a writer and researcher on self-development and the line manager as developer. He has written *A Manager's Guide to Coaching, Self-development: A Facilitator's Guide, Human Resource Development* in the Fast-track MBA series, *The Line Manager as Developer* and the *Developing the Developers* research report. He consults and researches in blue chip companies, and public and voluntary organizations. He is a director of the European Mentoring Centre and an elected Council member of AMED, and has been Associate Head of Sheffield Business School and a National Assessor for the National Training Awards.

Innovation
& Creativity

JONNE CESERANI
& PETER GREATWOOD

OF

SYNECTICS®

Published in association with  AMED

KOGAN
PAGE

First published in 1995
Reprinted in 1996 (twice)

Kogan Page Limited
120 Pentonville Road
London N1 9JN

© Jonne Ceserani and Peter Greatwood, 1995

Some of the material in the Toolkit section of this book was previously published in *The Innovator's Handbook* by Vincent Nolan (Sphere Books, 1989) and is reproduced here with his agreement. Mr Nolan was the founder and former Chairman of Synectics Ltd.

British Library Cataloguing in Publication Data

A CIP record for this book is available from the British Library.

ISBN 0 7494 1593 2

Printed and bound in Great Britain by Clays Ltd, St Ives plc

Contents

Part One
The Toolkit

You already know everything within these pages
— you just do not know you know it.

You already know more than is in these pages —
you only need to use it.

You will add to what is in these pages as you
work to discover.

you are creative

you are an innovator

take this thought **into yourself**

I ☞ am creative

I ☞ am an innovator

I now choose to be creative and innovative

This is not a book, it is a prompt to a journey of
exploration. If you do no more than read the
pages you are unlikely to get real value from
your experience.

Introduction

This is a **'not-a-book'**.

We realise you may have been fooled into believing it is a book, because it has pages, a cover, an ISBN number, and other things that are book like.

When we were invited to write this one of our colleagues said, "Oh no, not another 'how to...' book, they never work."

We agreed with him. In our experience many 'how to...' books are rather turgid and difficult to use.

This is a **'not-a-book'**, where the printed pages are our medium for prompting, telling and guiding. The other elements are your mind and the minds of everyone else you involve in your experience.

The journey is all of these elements brought together.

We hope you enjoy the journey and get many rewards from the experience now and in the future.

We use the behaviours, tools and maps described in this book ourselves. They help us to be successful in our endeavour, sometimes, and we try and use them to learn from our mistakes.

They are not the **right way**, and however you choose to use your learning from this journey is fine if it helps you make progress in whatever tasks you face.

If you simply try and apply what you find in this book as a formula solution, probably nothing will happen and you will decide it does not work.

This '**not-a-book**' introduces several paradoxes.

Paradoxically, creativity and innovation are about freedom and play, yet structure is essential if you are to be free.

We spend years building up expertise in order to have a place in society, yet experts can be the most difficult people to involve in a creative session. Experts think they know the answer and if you are in the process of innovating, the answer is unknown until you finish.

The TQM movement, over the recent years, has encouraged people in companies to **get it right first time** and **do it once, do it right**. Slogans more appropriate to innovation might be **get it wrong, but for goodness sake do something different** or **do it as many times as possible and see how much you learn**.

The paradox is about doing the latter **and** making progress and staying in business while you do it.

During an innovation session that was considering new toilet cleaning products, one of the participants expressed a wish:

> 'I wish we could get snails to walk around the toilet bowl eating the dirt as they went.'

This wish was used to develop new thinking about getting enzymes to 'eat' the dirt. And in this way a new toilet cleaner with enzymes was invented.

Innovation is the central issue in economic prosperity

Michael Porter Harvard Business School

Everything that can be invented has been invented

Charles H Duell Director of US Patent Office 1899

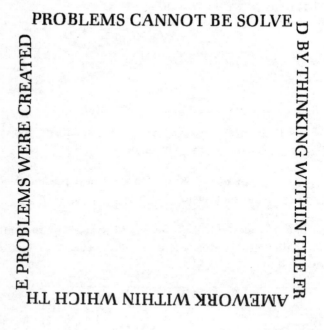

PROBLEMS CANNOT BE SOLVED BY THINKING WITHIN THE FRAMEWORK WITHIN WHICH THE PROBLEMS WERE CREATED

Albert Einstein

The case of tape recording revelation

We were in conversations with a large company attempting to persuade them to license our problem-solving procedures as part of one of their courses. Their four managers at the meeting claimed that their present problem-solving system was satisfactory and they did not need ours.

We said that we had analysed their procedures and there were some problems with them. To demonstrate this, we suggested that they use their system to solve a problem. We had a tape recorder with us and we would tape the proceedings, take them through our analysis and then they could decide whether or not our process might be useful.

They called in two more of their staff to make a group of six, and tackled the problem of a loss-proof stopper for a wide-mouthed vacuum flask. (No strings, chains, or hinges were acceptable because marketing tests showed them to be unpopular.)

When they reviewed the tape with us identifying actions that tended to block ideas, they asked us to stop after 10 minutes and decided to redesign their procedures, incorporating our processes.

In the beginning was the word:

SYNECTICS®

the bringing together of diverse elements

When the people who founded our business in the early 1960s tried to describe what they did, they realised that no existing word could sum it up. So they created a new word which became our trademark .

Today, Synectics® is the name of our firm, the brand name of the services we offer in managing the creative process, and a technique that is used by many businesses worldwide.

We made the word up from the Greek **syn** and **ectos** which together suggest **'the bringing together of diversity'**.

This is a fundamental element of our approach to facilitating innovative thinking. It is also the cornerstone characteristic of high-performing organizations.

This not-a-book is designed for you, to help you on a journey that provides an opportunity for sharing some of our experience.

This not-a-book is in three parts.

You can read them in any order. If you like the big picture first you might want to start with Part Two. Part One is about the detail behind the big picture. If you wish to experiment first and check your experience against ours, you could begin with Part Three.

Part One is about a toolkit of processes that we find helpful.

Part Two describes a map for helping to explore the territory of innovation.

Part Three is a series of questions to you, the reader, to help you explore your territory and that of others you interact with.

Innovation in Business — the Big Picture

In 1993 Synectics® carried out some research about innovation in major businesses in the USA. Similar findings come out of research by the Department of Trade and Industry in the UK.

Our report, **Succeeding at Innovation**, reveals a gap between what leading corporations say about innovation and what they do.

The gap is large.

- **80 per cent** of US companies say that innovation is very important to their business.

- Only **4 per cent** say they are good at it.

These are clear indications of a consistent connection between a company's commitment to innovation and its success in the marketplace.

Findings in four categories support this contention:

Sales

Sales increase in highly innovative companies was nearly twice as great as in those which were less innovative. The more innovative companies reported an average increase of 10.8 per cent, while the least innovative companies reported only 5.7 per cent.

Profits

Profit increase in the most innovative companies was more than three times as great as in less innovative companies; the more innovative reported an average profit increase of 51 per cent against just 14 per cent for the less innovative.

Market share

Market share increase for the more innovative companies was more than twice as great; they reported a 50 per cent increase in market share growth, compared to only 27 per cent increase in less innovative companies.

Innovation budget

More than twice as many highly innovative companies have a specific budget for innovation compared with the less innovative companies.

The report recommends five basic strategies to improve a company's chances for becoming a high-performing and successful organization:

1. **Make meetings more productive.**
2. **Institute formal innovation programmes or expand existing ones.**
3. **Seek ideas from outside sources.**
4. **Foster improved teamwork and communication.**
5. **Understand the future needs of consumers/customers.**

One of our colleagues expressed the view that we should not publish these five recommendations because they are too simple, so will be discounted.

We offered an alternative view. The report is telling us how easy it is to begin to change the way we work, to tap our own creative potential and allow our colleagues to do the same.

The opportunity to get creative, and be more innovative, lies dormant within every organization.

The Innovation Quotient questionnaire on the next three pages will help you identify yourself.

Are you a **spectator**, a **seeker**, or a **star**?

The IQ — Innovation Quotient

Creativity and Innovation questionnaire

Circle the number matching your opinion in relation to the following questions:

1. How well do the leaders in different functional areas in your organization work together?

   Not well at all   2 4 6 8 10   Very well

2. How effectively does your organization break down barriers between different functional areas so that ideas can be exchanged?

   Not well at all   1 2 3 4 5   Very well

3. Does your organization have a formal approach for generating ideas and using creativity/innovation to address business issues?

   Don't have it   1 3 5 7 9   Have it and
                                             use it

4. How often do meetings at your company produce truly innovative results?

   Never   2 4 6 8 10   Always

5. Does your company's mission statement specifically mention creativity and/or innovation?

   No   0 5   Yes

6. How would you rate your organization's actual performance in making innovation happen?

   Need to   1 2 3 4 5   Superior at
   learn basics   innovation

7. How successful is your company in developing new products and getting them to market?

   Not successful   1 2 3 4 5   Very successful
   at all

8. Does your organization have a budget for innovation?

   There is no   2 4 6 8 10   There is a
   budget today   clearly
                                          specified budget

9. Do you have formal programmes for innovation in your organization?

   Not at all   1 2 3 4 5   Widely

10. To what extent do you have quantified goals for innovation and its impact on future performance?

    Difficult to   1 2 3 4 5   A number of
    connect to any   goals link to it
    quantified goals   directly

11. How important do people see innovation to be in their day-to-day jobs?

    Not important   1 2 3 4 5   Important

12. How well are champions of innovation supported in driving projects through to implementation?

    Not well at all 1 2 3 4 5   Very well

13. Are senior people able to take risks?

    Not at all   1 2 3 4 5   Yes

14. To what extent is innovation celebrated and rewarded?

    Hardly at all   1 2 3 4 5   A great deal

15. To what degree do senior management encourage innovation by demonstrating that "It's okay to fail"?

    Hardly at all   1 2 3 4 5   A great deal

16. How well do senior executives demonstrate commitment to innovation in the face of high short-term pressure?

    Not well at all   1 2 3 4 5   Very well

17. How well are champions of innovation supported overall within your organization?

    Not well at all   2 4 6 8 10   Very well

18. To what extent are you open to learning from competitors and other industries?

    Not at all   1 2 3 4 5   Very open

19. To what extent are your innovation projects managed by cross-functional teams?

    Rarely   1 2 3 4 5   Almost always

20. How well does your organization recognize and exploit the diversity of people's talents?

    Not well at all   1 2 3 4 5   Very well

Calculate your Innovation Quotient by adding your scores. Use this scale:

    Less than 55 = Spectators
    55–84 = Seekers
    85 or more = Stars

a structure for fostering creativity in individuals and teams

Stepping off the Cliff

Making the decision to do things differently, to use your own creativity, and that of a team, to try and be innovative can be likened to stepping off a cliff.

Normal life is comfortable, or at least you can make some sense of it, even if it is not perfect. Innovation is about stepping into the unknown.

> **If you think about things the way you always have thought about them you will get what you always got.**

> **To do new things it is essential to think in new ways.**

Whenever we are working with a new group in an innovation session we tell them:

> **Expect to be confused. We will deliberately generate a creative fog, a place where nothing makes rational sense, and ideas and perspectives are different. If you apply reason to this too soon you will be going back to what you know and no innovation will take place.**

This is a very frightening notion. In a business it is also apparently crazy. After all, decisions have to be made or we will all get fired.

You will recognize some of the phases of projects in which you have been involved in the diagram opposite which describes the anatomy of innovation.

The anatomy of innovation

A map of the organizational energy during any major transition programme

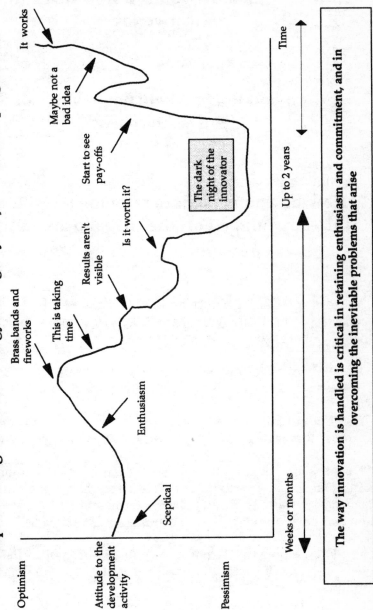

Optimism

Attitude to the development activity

Pessimism

Brass bands and fireworks

This is taking time

Results aren't visible

Is it worth it?

Enthusiasm

Sceptical

Start to see pay-offs

Maybe not a bad idea

It works

The dark night of the innovator

Weeks or months

Up to 2 years

Time

The way innovation is handled is critical in retaining enthusiasm and commitment, and in overcoming the inevitable problems that arise

How do you allow yourself to take off into this creative fog?

How do you know where to go when all about you seems chaos?

How do you make it to safety when you have already jumped off the cliff and are falling?

35 years ago George Prince and Bill Gordon recognized that it is focusing on **how** you work that allows you to make choices when **what** you are working on is confusion.

To be innovative and tap into people's creativity you need **a process structure to tell you where to go next**.

The underlying model should be a creative problem-solving process that can be applied to consideration of anything new.

The problem-solving kite opposite began life as a diamond, with an equal space top and bottom. It has become a kite because most businesses claim they can get ideas. Selecting which ones to work on and developing these into actions is where they ask for help.

The kite demonstrates that most effort is needed in the bottom half of the model, and it is a cycle of activity to take you forward gradually.

Problem-solving process

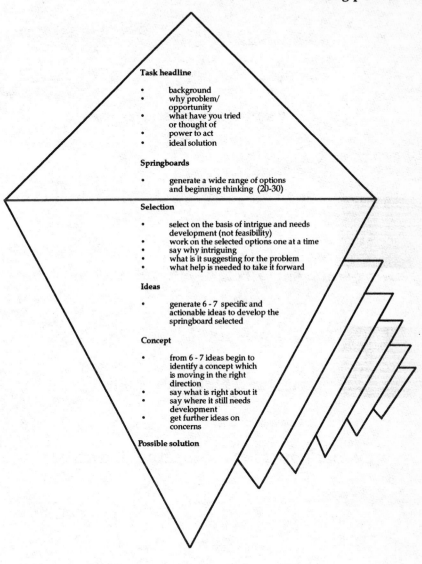

Task headline

- background
- why problem/ opportunity
- what have you tried or thought of
- power to act
- ideal solution

Springboards

- generate a wide range of options and beginning thinking (20-30)

Selection

- select on the basis of intrigue and needs development (not feasibility)
- work on the selected options one at a time
- say why intriguing
- what is it suggesting for the problem
- what help is needed to take it forward

Ideas

- generate 6 - 7 specific and actionable ideas to develop the springboard selected

Concept

- from 6 - 7 ideas begin to identify a concept which is moving in the right direction
- say what is right about it
- say where it still needs development
- get further ideas on concerns

Possible solution

Establishing Environments for Creativity: Cultural Considerations

Set some expectations

by

gaining some shared clarity about how to picture
the world

and

agreeing how to work together to succeed

and

going to the right place to take risks

Cycling Worlds

You spend most of your time in an **operational world**.

It is a world associated with doing routine activities, in learned or programmed ways. You base your decisions on procedures or rules and expect to experience successful outcomes, which you normally do.

Driving a car is a common example. Mostly you arrive in one piece. Manufacturing in a production line is associated with a repetitive set of processes that uses a common set of inputs to manufacture a stream of identical products. Office administrative procedures are another example.

When routine activities go wrong you normally resolve the issue by a process of analysis and linear reasoning until you identify the problem. You solve it by implementing known alternative solutions or procedures.

This is a focused, blinkered, way of working, which is perfectly fine, providing you continue to experience successful outcomes.

What are you to do if you begin to experience a failure of existing solutions, including the known alternatives?

What if you experience success and also see that new opportunities could be identified?

A different way of working is needed and you will have to cross over into the **innovation world**.

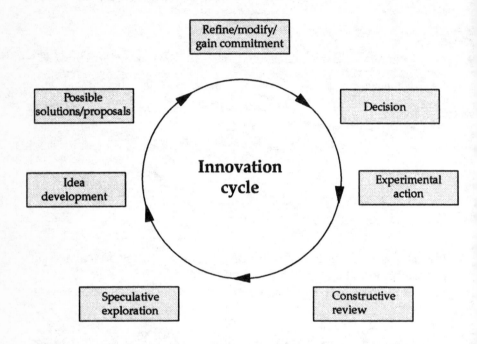

This is a place where you will suspend your normal way of working and behave very differently.

Speculative exploration is necessary in order for something new to be imagined. For years the birds flew around in the sky and nobody acknowledged this, birds just did it.

One day someone must have looked up and acknowledged this.

> **"I wish I could fly like the birds, that looks really great,
> I wonder how they do that?"**

Someone has to speculate like this to provide a view into a possible future so you can have an idea and engage in some idea development.

> **"I see they flap their wings. I will flap my arms and see if I
> can fly. That didn't work. I know, I'll tie banana leaves to
> my arms, they're rather like feathers. Hmmm, that doesn't
> work but I feel some resistance against the air, let me think
> about this some more..."**

You could have been that person. You speculated, had an idea, and tried it as a possible solution.

Clearly, since it does not work further activity will be needed to **refine or modify the idea**.

Then you can try some further **experimental action**.

In order to learn from failure you will want to engage in **constructive evaluation**.

This cycle of activity is dramatically different from the **operational world**. The latter is associated with tunnel vision and focus on task to the exclusion of other interference. The **innovation world** needs an open mind, fun-loving and childlike behaviour.

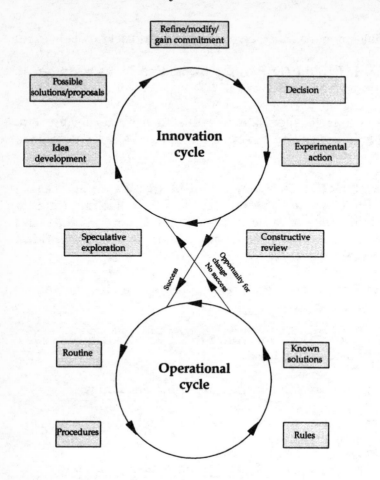

In a business these two worlds are constantly in conflict.

● Operational thinking is about **now,** and **knowing the answer.**

● Innovative thinking is about **the future** and **not knowing.**

If we make suggestions to you with our innovation head on about how you can run your business differently, and you are thinking operationally, you will be able to tell us why all our suggestions will not work. You will probably be right as well, and the conversation will be pointless.

Innovation World

Agree to step into the innovation world together

Life is a process of cycling between both worlds

You can only work in one at a time

It is impossible to be in both simultaneously

Creating the Climate

If you live in a climate where your life is constantly under threat, you will spend much of your time and energy thinking about self defence and how to preserve your life.

If you set out to sail across an ocean to another land your activities will be focused on sailing the boat, plotting a course, and enjoying the experience.

When the boat hits an old wreck and starts to sink, your focus will change and all of your energy will be directed towards the immediate task of staying alive.

Businesses are like this. In order to move into an **innovation world** you will need to consider your climate, or culture.

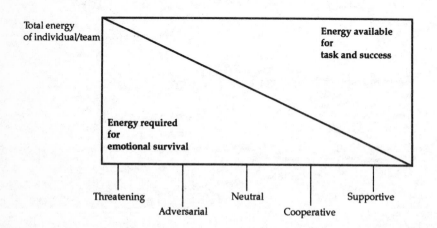

Climate

An individual, or team, has an amount of energy to give to doing some work. When it is all gone you will fall over and sleep, or die.

If you operate in an **adversarial** or **threatening** way, or if this is how people behave towards you, your energy, or that of the team, will be directed towards self-preservation.

Adversarial behaviour includes:

● pulling rank
● failing to pay attention or listen to others
● ignoring someone
● cross-examining opinions with challenging questions

Threatening behaviour includes:

● discounting or putting down other people's opinions
● openly challenging ideas
● reacting negatively or cynically to other people's views
● preaching and moralizing
● anger and threats of violence

You will probably recognize when you have been on either the receiving or giving ends of this style of working together.

The **innovation world** can only thrive when you strive to operate at the other end of this spectrum.

Working cooperatively or supportively removes the need for self-protection and team members are able to focus on task and success.

The open, childlike, playful mind needed for innovation can only blossom when the need to defend yourself has been removed.

It is also a more pleasant place to be, for you and your colleagues, and you get more work done.

Positive behaviours

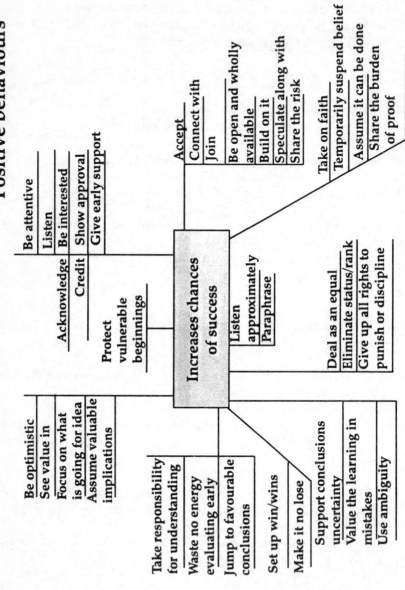

Increases chances of success

Be attentive
- Listen
- Be interested
- Show approval
- Give early support

Acknowledge
- Credit

Protect vulnerable beginnings

Accept
- Connect with
- Join
- Be open and wholly available
- Build on it
- Speculate along with
- Share the risk

Take on faith
- Temporarily suspend belief
- Assume it can be done
- Share the burden of proof

Listen approximately
- Paraphrase

Deal as an equal
- Eliminate status/rank
- Give up all rights to punish or discipline

Be optimistic
- See value in
- Focus on what is going for idea
- Assume valuable implications

Take responsibility for understanding

Waste no energy evaluating early

Jump to favourable conclusions

Set up win/wins

Make it no lose

Support conclusions uncertainty

Value the learning in mistakes

Use ambiguity

Negative behaviours

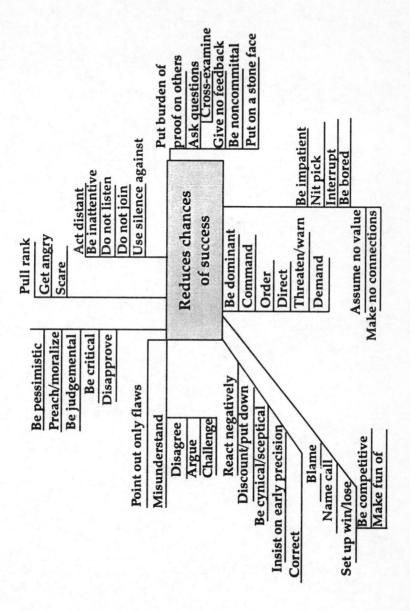

Innovation World

Bask in success

It is more fun

and

more productive

than

burning up

The case of the critical attitude

An invention group at a manufacturer of bandages and non-woven cloth developed a concept for making material that was so radical that they were not able to evaluate it for practicality. They did not know if it could be done. Altering the facts to protect their confidentiality, it was as though they had devised a system for programming a plant so that instead of growing leaves, it would grow garments — say socks.

They wanted to take the concept to the person in their company who was most expert in the area of the idea. One member said, 'Norm knows everything about this area, but he tends to react like most experts and spot all the reasons why it can't be done.'

They put their heads together and invented a way of presenting it that would shift Norm's usual attitude. They would present it as a rumour they had heard that the Russians had developed and successfully implemented this concept.

They reported that it worked beautifully. When they told Norm about it, he reacted with excitement and immediately began to speculate about how they might have overcome some of the difficulties.

Taking Risks, Failing and Being OK

You have probably read slogans developed for total quality programmes like:

'Do it once do it right'   **'Right first time'**

The same companies often say about themselves **'we are risk takers'**, and **'our employees are empowered to experiment with new ideas'** — providing they get it right first time of course!

We know of a company that tried to spread all four of the messages above, usually in the same breath. They are contradictory and belong in different worlds.

In the **operational world** it is appropriate to expect people to perform a task correctly and to make a minimum of errors. It is about doing what we know, in a way we understand, for a predictable outcome.

You now know that it is impossible to enter the **innovation world** unless you are able to **speculate, and experiment**.

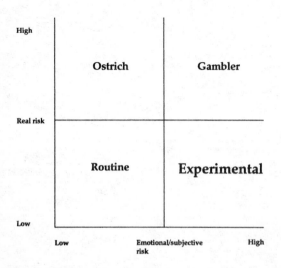

Real risk is when it actually hurts if you fail. When jumping off a cliff there is a real risk you will get hurt when you hit the ground.

Emotional risk is the nervous feeling of excitement when you are not sure about an outcome, like stage fright.

Gamblers take real risks. Consistent losses lead to bankruptcy. Gambling is exciting, therefore highly emotionally charged. Gambling is a place where knowing the outcomes so that you can measure the risk, the odds, is important.

Not a safe place for innovation.

Clerks are operating in routine ways delivering routine known outcomes.

Not a safe place for innovation.

Ostriches, by tradition, operate with their heads buried in the sand. This is a dangerous place to be. It feels safe, yet danger may lurk nearby. The entrepreneur, possibly an engineer with a successful new product he produces from his garage, may feel very successful. Although an excellent engineer, maybe his skills do not include finance, so he is not aware of growing receivables that are taking him towards bankruptcy. He is amazed when the bank manager arrives to foreclose on his mortgage.

Not a safe place for innovation.

The **experimenter** is able to innovate, to take risks, make mistakes, fail, and continue. An experimenter is safe because he or she is minimizing the real risk of failure, and the excitement of learning and experimenting provides the energy and drive to continue.

If you set out to develop a new explosive it is best done in a test tube. The mistakes will be survivable.

Innovation World

Go to a new place, mentally or physically

develop a climate and a way of working

minimize the real risk

so that you can

play

have fun

get it wrong

try again

Working in an Environment for Creativity

To **innovate**

you will be present in an environment full of

listening

speaking

evaluating

questioning

To raise and maintain high probabilities of success you know this will need to happen in a supportive and cooperative manner.

The Death of the Chairperson

This is a popular concept in many businesses, but may get you into trouble. The idea behind the idea will give you an opportunity to build supportive and cooperative meeting climates, essential for innovation to occur.

The chair is often the most senior person in the room, ultimately the decision maker, even if others apparently get a chance to make the right decision first before being overruled. The chair chooses who speaks, decides on agendas, directs the contents of the minutes, and acts the parent as necessary.

Not so far from the truth in many cases, this is also a description of two quite different roles, both of which one person can do to a degree, and neither is done well unless you can focus on one at a time.

One role is concerned with **content**, the task that is being worked on. The second role is focused on the **processes of how people are working together**.

This is somewhat analogous to a football referee. He never kicks the ball, this is for the players. Left to their own devices they would get in each other's way, even given a set of rules to play to.

Pause here and consider how simple the game of football is, compared to a business meeting, especially one where new ideas and decisions are being discussed.

Why is it then that we only consider playing football once we have a set of 'rules' **and a referee**, yet people will calmly venture into all manner of highly complex business meetings with no thought to **how they are going to work together and who is going to control it all**.

In the early days of our research we noticed how quickly people in groups get in each other's way, not always intentionally. It became clear that establishing the three roles described below dramatically improves the productivity of the group.

The role of the chairperson is in effect eliminated, and split to become two roles, **facilitator** and **problem owner**.

Facilitator

- Concerned with process only, never involved in content.
- Sets positive climate by:
  - accepting all ideas
  - writing down headlines of ideas, and solutions
  - giving everyone a chance to contribute.
- Elicits the ideas hidden behind questions.
- Manages the time and pace of the meeting.
- Ensures the problem owner's best current thinking is shared with the group.
- Ensures that everybody takes notes of what is in their mind.

Problem owner

- Owns the issue.
- Describes it.
- Directs the content of the meeting by:
  - contributing wishes and ideas, selecting the avenues to explore, paraphrasing ideas to check understanding before evaluating
  - evaluating constructively
  - deciding when a solution has been reached
  - committing to next action.

The third role is that of **resource**.

Resource

- Generates ideas.
- Makes suggestions.
- Generates solutions.
- Gives opinions only when they are asked for.

Next time you get together in a meeting, ask everyone to state their role. If more than two people think they are the problem owner you need to get this clear first. Our instant test is to see who will get fired, if the problem is not resolved. This is the problem owner. If they are not in the room your probability of implementing innovation has just gone down.

The case of the created opportunity

A manager who had repeatedly used innovation groups was given a 'dead end' assignment. His company was in the paper business and their mills used great quantities of electricity. He was put in charge of the Energy and Environment Department. This was before the energy crunch of 1974, and the department was considered to be a kind of police department to enforce government regulations.

This manager did not see it that way. Instead of being enforcers, he and his staff became enablers. He developed roving teams that visited all the company's installations to run innovation sessions with local groups, to invent ways to increase productivity and reduce energy use while complying with regulations. By the time he left a few years later, Energy and Environment was credited with inventing new ways of operating that had saved the company more than $85 million.

Listening: for Ideas and to the Meeting in your Head

When you were at school, how often did you spend time in your own little world, staring into space or out of the window?

Perhaps you rejoined the class when the board rubber made contact with your head, or the teacher screamed **'pay attention!'** at you.

Now that you attend business meetings, how often do you suddenly come to with a start and recognize that your attention has wandered?

Possibly your efforts to pay attention mean that when your chance to speak arrives you have forgotten what you wanted to say, or you will interrupt to avoid forgetting.

This describes experiences common to all of us. While someone speaks, or while you are reading this page, your mind will constantly be stimulated into thoughts of its own.

The thoughts you have will sometimes be clearly connected to the subject, or maybe they will have no obvious connection and you will be thinking, **'Why did I think that?'**

Once your mind has been stimulated you will tend to give your attention to this 'meeting' in your head, often more interesting than the public one in the room. You will **'drop out'**.

Your attention wanders (or wonders), and then you get hit on the head with the board rubber.

The following pattern of listening emerges:

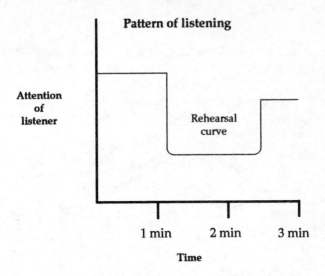

Your mind is a vast store of experiences and data. If I asked you to tell me everything you know you are unlikely to be able to do this. Much of your personal database is in your subconscious mind.

The thoughts that you have when you are 'out' of the public meeting are a major source of ideas.

A typical speaking rate is 150–200 words, yet your mind processes words at closer to 800–1000 per minute. Therefore, your mind has the capacity to produce many thoughts, many ideas, while someone is speaking.

You were taught at school to listen so you could understand, to pay attention. This is appropriate in some circumstances.

You had a natural aptitude to listen to the meeting in your head and let your mind wander, which has now been disciplined out of you. This is the skill to relearn.

Remember how to be a child.

If you are invited to have ideas it is not necessary to pay attention, better to let your mind wander so that it can tell you about the ideas it has.

A technique called **in/out listening** will help you manage the meeting in your head so that you can use your mind for ideas.

Create a new listening pattern like this:

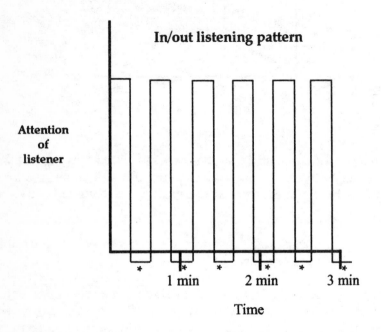

In/out listening pattern

Attention of listener

1 min   2 min   3 min

Time

Divide your note pad page into two columns (see opposite).

On the left make lecture notes.

On the right make notes about thoughts, associations, connections and images, etc. Draw pictures if you wish.

When you are listening to the public meeting, make lecture notes.

When your attention level falls and you are listening to your head, make notes in the right-hand column.

The trick to learn is to avoid censorship and record your first thought, whatever it is. Often these thoughts may be ridiculous, impossible, rude, illegal, or immoral. Try and avoid 'improving' them, gather the first thought.

It is yours and you do not have to share it, that will be your choice.

You will also find that this technique overcomes any tendency you may have to forget what it was you wanted to say, and it avoids the need to interrupt other people.

Him/her:	Me:
Lecture type notes of what the speaker is saying	Notes of my own connections, images, associations, thoughts and ideas

Speaking for Easy Listening — Giving Ideas or Opinions

Many of us are accustomed to giving our opinions and ideas in an environment where, frequently, every word is greeted with criticism. Unfortunately, such an environment is the norm for many business meetings.

Think for a moment about some of your recent experiences.

Were you interrupted with a comment before you had time to finish what you were saying? How often is the response to your words something like

● 'Yes, very interesting, but…', or

● 'I hear what you say, but…'?

So often, the response to your words is some level of attack, and you naturally defend yourself from this. A pattern for expressing ideas or opinions frequently looks like this:

Preamble

Idea or opinion

Wrap-up

You may begin with a preamble, preparing the ground for the idea and checking out the reception it is going to get. You then slip in the idea, and quickly, before it can be criticized, sell it.

The wrap-up is designed to ensure everyone is absolutely clear about what a good idea you have expressed.

This process for speaking is time consuming, because of the high potential for 'waffle'.

Additionally, the idea may be lost because your audience has given up listening to you. Remember the **in/out listening** described earlier, and you will see how many of your audience may be listening to the meeting in their head, rather than you.

Now you know why the level of misunderstanding is so high in many meetings. Frequently nobody heard what you actually said, only a version that was sort of related.

Headline and background is an alternative approach that will help you overcome the problem highlighted above.

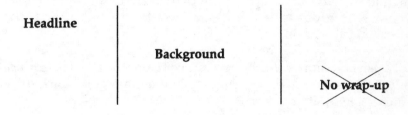

Headline

Background

No wrap-up

Preface your ideas and opinions with a headline that positions the thought in the mind of the audience, like a newspaper headline. Follow the headline with some words of background that fill in a little of what you are thinking. There is no need to sell your viewpoint because this adds nothing to it. If your colleagues are using **in/out listening** they can use the background as a trigger to further thoughts.

Questioning ... the Wisdom?

Getting the right balance between information and creativity

Think about the last time somebody invited you to help them by giving some ideas. **Did you give an idea or did you ask a question?**

If we put any group of people in a room in order to do some creative problem solving, and the problem owner describes the problem, almost without exception the participants will begin to ask questions, **in order to get more information so that they fully understand the problem**.

This wish for more information is positively meant. The group wants to be able to help the problem owner, therefore they wish to understand the problem.

Think about how you feel when operating in a fog of misunderstanding. Not very comfortable because you may get it wrong?

The problem owner can be pictured as a person in a hole in the ground. They are surrounded with so much information they are unable to see any new directions to move in.

A group, unencumbered with all this information, has the possibility of offering new perspectives.

They can pass down a ladder leading to new thoughts and possibilities.

The alternative is that the group ask lots of questions until they know as much as the problem owner about the problem, and you are all in the hole together.

This can be very comforting for the problem owner, but you, the resource, have lost much of your ability to help.

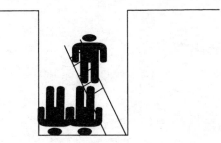

You do not need as much information as you thought in order to give ideas.

Stay naïve!!

Children often have the interesting ideas because they do not know. **They guess**. Do some guessing and you will generate unusual perspectives. If you are truly looking to innovate you cannot know the answer before you arrive — so who can say what is right or wrong?

In an innovation meeting do not ask questions during the early stages of the problem definition and idea generation.

This comes as a surprise to you perhaps? Try it and enjoy it!

Think for a moment

about the number of reasons you ask questions

and

why questions are asked of you.

List them here.

We want to focus your attention on two aspects:

the destructive nature of questions

and

hiding ideas behind questions

How they affect the climate of the innovation meeting

The Destructive Nature of Questions

You may have drawn up a long list. Some of the reasons are 'legitimate' in the sense that they are questions asked for a genuine wish for the answer.

Others lack this 'legitimacy', in that they are designed to demonstrate your personal superiority, or someone else's stupidity.

We are not suggesting you use all of these reasons yourself, you will know the ones you use and why. However, it is clear that questions are used for many purposes.

You may have had the experience where someone has asked a question, the answer is given, and the response from the questioner is:

   'No, no! That's not what I meant at all...'

The respondent apparently got it wrong...and is feeling stupid and defensive because of this. He or she has been discounted!

Actually what has happened is that the respondent guessed the wrong question from that long list of reasons why questions are asked. He or she gave the right answer to the wrong question, and is made to feel bad because of it.

Feeling bad is an inappropriate place to be in a climate that is designed to nurture innovation. If you are going to ask a question in your innovation sessions, say what is behind the question and take away the need for guessing.

Hiding Ideas behind Questions

A colleague of ours was running an innovation session where the problem concerned a scum that formed on top of a brew. This fell into the brew and destroyed the flavour.

The following question was asked:

  'What temperature does the vat operate at?'

The answer was given as so many degrees by the problem owner and the session continued.

During a break the questioner was overheard by the problem owner talking to a colleague. He was saying what a pity it was about the vat temperature because given an increase of x degrees there is a chemical that would form the scum into a biscuit that could be lifted off.

The problem owner became excited, saying that the vat temperature was not that critical and could be changed so that the chemical could be used.

The idea was there all the time, and did not get into the innovation session because the resource asked a question instead of giving the idea.

How many ideas exist in you, and your organization, that are hidden because questions are asked instead of ideas being given?

Discounting and Revenge Cycles: How to Assume Positive Intent

Think about an occasion when you were in a meeting and somebody criticized somebody else's opinion or idea. The person who was criticized went quiet, and next contributed to the meeting when they spotted an opportunity to get back at the first person.

This often then develops into a game of tennis, each attempting to score points over the other. In most large corporations there will be at least one pair, frequently among senior management, who go to a meeting in order to play revenge cycles, never to get any work done.

Often this **discounting** of another person's opinions and ideas is unintentional. Given that this is the case, it is difficult for the discounter to change their behaviour because they do not recognize that they are generating effects that they do not intend.

As the person feeling offended after being discounted, you can **choose to let the effect on you be positive rather than negative**.

Next time some one criticizes your opinion try this technique. Respond with something like:

> 'That is a very different view from mine. I would be interested to explore where we are agreeing and where we differ...'

You will need to find a form of words that is natural to you. The difference in the interaction that follows will be quite dramatically different from your normal experience.

It may need the faith and commitment of a saint to do this and it will not be easy. You also have to mean it. If you are cynical about it, it will not work.

George Prince, one of the founders of Synectics®, considers **assuming positive intent** as the single most powerful dynamic which can be introduced to meetings, in order to build the supportive climate needed for innovation.

Play the discounting game.

Get into a pair or group of three with any friends or colleagues. One of you begins to wax lyrical to the other(s) about something you have heard, seen or experienced recently that you thought was really terrific.

The other(s) should discount the speaker in as many ways as possible.

Discounts are in three categories:

● **oral** — That's crap!

● **tonal** — Really? (said in an obviously cynical tone)

● **non-verbal** — falling asleep

You will be really good at this. Everyone discounts a lot, often without realizing we are doing it. Talk about the effect this is having on one another.

A message for everyone who chooses to discount deliberately, playing corporate politics.

We are all sensitive and that is how we are meant to be. If you are habitually poker faced and overly assertive at work, think about how you are when with your family or friends.

Which is most natural to you? Which is most fun? Which will be most helpful in an innovation meeting?

Open-minded

constructive

evaluation

Change is inevitable, progress is not.

Itemized Response

Itemized response is a process for protecting ideas.

Think about how you respond to new ideas or opinions that are offered to you, and how others respond when you make the offers.

Speculation and new ideas are like babies, easily hurt and destroyed unless you protect them. Given the right environment within which to grow and develop, stunning results are achieved.

Often groups evaluate ideas by saying only what is wrong, and the level of criticism or evaluation is so general that it is useless as a guide as to how to improve the thinking.

The **itemized response** process itemizes, as a series of headlines, the evaluation of an idea or set of circumstances.

You begin by **listing the pluses**, or positive aspects of the idea.

Many times, potentially valuable thinking is never recognized as such because sufficient time is not given to working through the pluses for the idea.

Listing pluses is, in itself, a building process.

Using **in/out listening**, additional pluses will be triggered and suddenly an idea can blossom.

After the pluses have been listed, move on to look at the **areas of concern** that need to be addressed — do not think of it as what is wrong.

List these as headlines using a problem-solving focus like:

● **How to...**

● **I wish...**

● **I need a way...**

This form of words establishes what needs to happen for the idea to improve, and sets you up with problem-solving statements to work with creatively.

If you believe something is too expensive and simply say so — 'It is too expensive!', this leaves very limited options for where to go next. Too expensive is a shut out. Many members of the group will simply stop thinking about implementing the idea.

Turning this into a more positive focus will dramatically change the perspective of the group.

Maybe you are thinking, 'I like the solution **and** my issue is:

● how to do this with cheaper raw materials

● how to use different budgets

● I need a way to do this over two years

● I wish we could find cheaper labour.

All of these statements are versions of 'too expensive' type thinking. They are more specific, however, and we can now address the issues using creative problem solving.

The Creative Problem-solving Structure

You could regard using a structured process to be creative and innovative as a contradiction.

On the one hand the interest is to encourage free thinking, minimal barriers, no judgement, open-minded evaluation, yet...

...as you will discover, we are offering a prescriptive structure, including the language to use during the process.

Problem-solving process

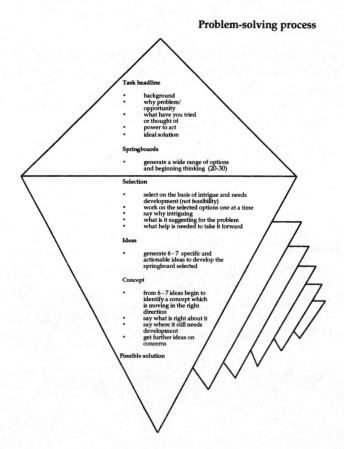

Task headline
- background
- why problem/ opportunity
- what have you tried or thought of
- power to act
- ideal solution

Springboards
- generate a wide range of options and beginning thinking (20-30)

Selection
- select on the basis of intrigue and needs development (not feasibility)
- work on the selected options one at a time
- say why intriguing
- what is it suggesting for the problem
- what help is needed to take it forward

Ideas
- generate 6 - 7 specific and actionable ideas to develop the springboard selected

Concept
- from 6 - 7 ideas begin to identify a concept which is moving in the right direction
- say what is right about it
- say where it still needs development
- get further ideas on concerns

Possible solution

Our experience is that the **process structure** is a key element in allowing an individual or group to grope their way through the creative fog.

Just as we will offer you specific behaviours to allow you to work at **listening** and **being creative**, we offer specific behaviours for problem solving, along the lines of the kite model illustrated on the previous page.

We encourage you to follow the process, even if it seems rather bureaucratic initially. Our experience is that the alternative to a structured process is **unstructured debate** which leads to everyone getting lost.

A group of eight people is ideal for using this process. More than this and the group can become difficult to manage.

You can use the process alone if you wish.

A lot of useful work can be accomplished in an hour if you are looking merely to do some new thinking.

Problems that need breakthroughs will need a day or two at a time and possibly several meetings.

More of this in Part Two, How Innovation Works.

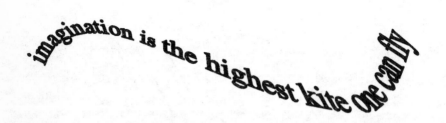

Planning

You cannot begin to work in different ways in isolation from other people, and others will not join you unless they know something of what they are in for.

Everything you have worked on so far in this book is about:

● setting expectations about experimenting

● establishing a climate to allow risk

● agreeing about supportive ways to work

You must do this with everyone you plan to include in your innovation programme.

Just like the analogy with football match we introduced earlier, agree the rules of the game. **Establish some ground rules or guidelines.**

Establish who the problem owner is, and if it is more than one person be clear that it really is a shared responsibility.

Ensure that you have the right players.

Choose the other participants, implementers of the potential solution, non-experts whose 'naïvety' will easily allow them to generate different perspectives (imagine a chef in a group of engineers?)

Task Analysis

The challenge is to give the group enough information to allow them to generate ideas, and not so much that they join you as problem owner in the hole.

Remember the discussion about the need for questions earlier.

Nothing in this process is right or wrong. You will need to judge what seems appropriate. Sometimes it will work well and other times not so well.

The following is a structure for talking about a problem to get you started.

1. Task headline
2. Background
3. Power to act
4. What has been tried and thought of before
5. The ideal solution

1   Task headline

You know about **headline and background** from earlier (see page 51).

Establish the **headline** for the problem and make it aspirational or directional.

Use language like:

● **How to...**

or

● **I wish...**

Both forms establish a view of the future and the language encourages ideas.

If the problem is that your current product portfolio does not appeal to the consumer and you open the session saying just that, you will probably only depress everyone.

Turn this into:

● **How can we find the products that will get our customers fighting to buy from us?**

or

● **I wish I could reach into the heads of our customers and get them to spill out their desires.**

In our experience, the group will be more inclined to wake up and start work given either of these alternatives.

2 *Background*

Describe a little of the background to the problem for the assembled group.

This is not so much to give information as to begin to trigger thoughts so people can have ideas.

Remember the **in/out listening process** described earlier (page 48). The group are listening to this task analysis in order to be triggered for novel thinking.

We are at the very beginning of trying to generate a creative fog in which to fumble about as we seek new solutions.

Sometimes, just for fun, get some groups to generate initial ideas **before** they know the problem. It is always possible to use a beginning idea to generate a further thought, if you choose to use it for that purpose. It proves how little you need to know before you can have useful thoughts in an innovative session. Nothing!

If the background goes on too long you will almost certainly end up with a long list of all the reasons the problem cannot be solved. Chances are the group will simply agree with you at this stage, in which case you may as well go home early.

The background is to stimulate the group. You can always add more information later as necessary, if it is still relevant.

Often, information that you thought was relevant loses this relevance because the new thinking that is taking you towards a possible solution does not depend on old   assumptions or constraints.

Why is it a problem for you? (the problem owner)

Maybe you are worried about your children and drugs, so you decide the problem is:

● How to solve the drugs problem

Given that the combined efforts of the police forces of the world have yet to crack this one, it is unlikely that you will be able to make any significant progress.

Why is it a problem for me? You are concerned about your children, therefore reframing the problem as:

● How to keep my children off drugs

is a different positioning that is more likely to give you some answers that you can use.

In business often the problems seem so big that it is difficult for an individual to conceive of making any progress. Reframing the issue at a more personal level often gives a place to begin problem solving.

Early answers mean you make progress and this builds the energy to continue and solve the problem in phases.

3 *Power to act*

It is important to generate solutions that can be acted on.

The whole process of innovation is ridiculed by some people because their only experience is of generating lots of impractical ideas that nobody can implement.

It is pointless to put a lot of effort into new thinking and then not have any power to implement the solution.

Thinking this through may lead you to make new decisions about who the problem owner is, or who to include in the problem-solving team.

4   *What has been tried and thought of before*

Often there are solutions around that would solve a problem if only you knew how to implement them.

Maybe somebody else does and your problem-solving task is easier than you thought.

Perhaps you know what you would like to do, or have some ideas about a possible direction and cannot bring them together into a solution. Maybe someone else can.

Clearly you are well into the balancing act between too much information and enough to avoid unnecessarily reinventing the wheel.

It may be that you already have a solution and you are using the group to test it, or seeing if they come up with the same answer, so that they feel more committed to the outcome.

If you are in this camp, tell everybody you have the answer and let people be innovative about something else.

5   *The ideal solution*

Imagine you have a magic wand and a wish.

Magic wands are really great, because you can do anything with them.

This is a key step at the beginning of any problem-solving session.

If you, as problem owner, wish for something that exists and could be done you leave no room for new thinking.

The word **wish** is used quite deliberately.

Wish for something beyond anything you believe possible and you open up a gap between where you are now and where you wish to be, if only...

This gap is the space for creativity and innovation. The responsibility for establishing it lies with you, as problem owner.

The case of the typewriter keys

The marketing vice-president of a large business machine company wanted to train a creative team that included engineers and salespeople. The manager of the typewriter division was 'asked' to send five of his engineers for a week's innovation training. He was reluctant to spare five of his people for a week, but was directed to do as requested.

On the Monday when the five engineers returned from the training he summoned them to his office and said, in effect, prove how creative you have become. For years the company had been troubled by untreated typewriter keys getting mixed with those that were heat treated. The raw keys wore out quickly and were the cause of complaints. Both treated and untreated keys looked the same. The manager asked the group to solve the problem.

The group went back to a meeting and held a session. By the end if the day they had developed a concept and tested it. During the heat treating process the keys could be given a tiny shot of radioactivity. At inspection time keys would be tested with a Geiger counter, and nonradioactive keys would be discarded.

The manager professed to be pleased, but he never got over his adversarial attitude toward the group. This was a case for the importance of discounts — the manager felt discounted by the way he was dealt with concerning his five engineers.

Springboards

Remember the example we introduced earlier. The birds flew around in the sky for years and years. One day someone must have looked up and thought:

'That looks really great, **I wish I could do that**. It must be wonderful to be able to fly.'

Until someone had that thought and expressed a desire to do something that was clearly unrealistic at the time, it was not possible to have ideas that could lead to the innovation of a human flying like the birds.

Of course, we do not fly like birds, we use aeroplanes. The ideas behind the original thought gave us the solution, not the speculation itself.

Springboards are the beginning thoughts that lead us to new thinking.

Ideas are specific and actionable thoughts that allow us to move towards possible solutions.

'I know, I will flap my arms like the birds. No that did not work... I know, I will fix banana leaves to my arms, they are like feathers. No, that does not work, but I am feeling a resistance against the air, let me continue to experiment...'

The **ideas** above are specific and actionable, not just speculative wishes.

*If at first the idea is not absurd,
then there is no hope for it*

Albert Einstein

Speculate when you need newness

Speculative thoughts, presented constructively, are labelled **springboards**.

You could liken them to the diving board in the swimming pool. At first you may nervously step off the end. As you gain confidence you take leaps, and when you do not get hurt you may somersault as well.

So it is with speculation. As you enjoy the freedom of letting your mind roam free, see where it will take you, if you allow it space.

Springboards can include:

● redefinitions of the task headline
● wishes
● starting ideas
● challenges to constraints on the problem
● random thoughts
● feeling or gut level reactions
● apparently conflicting points of view.

The purpose is to:

● open up the issue to new perspectives
● increase the range of options
● encourage speculation about future possibilities
● maintain a positive climate
● overcome the limiting effect of real world restrictions
● overcome the reluctance of non-experts to give ideas
● overcome the tendency of experts to want to be right
● encourage the use of speculative thinking.

Springboarding is turbo-charged brainstorming.

Normal judgement is suspended.

Do not ask questions or allow them to be asked, encourage people to guess.

Use **in/out listening** to hear everything spoken for what it suggests, not whether it is right or wrong.

Practise suspending judgement in your thinking as well as your speaking — not an easy thing to do initially. It will take practice.

Use **headlines** followed by **background** to express the springboards.

Capture the headlines on flipcharts so that the group can revel in their productivity.

Use language like:

● **How to...**

or

● **I wish...**

Both of these formats encourage positive thinking about possible new futures.

Speculative Thinking Exercise

The purpose of this exercise is to practise generating spring-boards. It is essential for the owner to get involved with generating springboards along with the resource.

To obtain maximum benefit from the exercise, keep strictly to the roles and follow the steps exactly.

Owner	Resource
1. States task headline and gives background information. Why a problem/opportunity for him/her. What tried and thought of. His/her power and willingness to act. What would he/she wish for.	1. Resource listens for ideas, makes notes of thoughts triggered, without judging their relevance. No questions!
2. Owner listens with an open mind to be triggered with additional wishes and ideas. No judgements.	2. Resource converts notes from in/out listening into springboards: usually headlined as How to .../ I wish ... statements

3. Owner and resource continue triggering from each other's springboards to go on generating a wide range of springboards about the issue.

The case of family involvement

The director of research of a large chemical company was questioning whether an innovation programme was really effective. He was asked to identify a difficult current problem and select an appropriate team of six non-trained people as Team A. Team B was made up of six people who had innovation skills and experience.

The problem they were given concerned a new combination fertilizer and weed killer. To be effective, the fields needed to be treated in the spring, before being planted. It was too late to demonstrate it for the following season. The teams were given several days to develop a marketing programme.

Team A developed a sound, conventional approach using laboratory-generated photographic evidence and printed descriptions of its efficacy.

Team B developed a programme that included the above and in addition a home demonstration kit for the farmer. It included a two-part window box, attractive and unusual flower seeds, and instructions for using soil from active growing fields. In one part the farmer would use the new combination product, and in the other the farm's usual fertilizer. In a few weeks they would have a persuasive demonstration of the product's efficacy.

The director of research loved Team B's more innovative and swifter response.

Imaging, Metaphor, Analogy and Excursion — Journeys into Absurdity

You have now experienced some of the freedom of **springboarding**. We described it as turbo-charged brainstorming, and now you are going to wind up the turbo charger.

To encourage the use of imaging, metaphor and analogy, the power that drives the turbo charger, Synectics® invented a process called **excursion**.

You will have had the experience many times in your life where something that you were unable to recall comes back to you at an apparently strange moment. Typically this is when driving, showering, shaving, putting on make-up, sleeping, etc.

What is happening is that your subconscious is working on the problem that you were unable to solve, without you interfering because you are now thinking about something else.

When it has something to tell you it does so.

Excursion is a process for doing this whenever you wish.

There are many excursions and you can invent as many more as you wish. They share a common structure.

● Do something to generate some thinking that is irrelevant to the problem you are trying to solve.

● Use this material to invent connections between the irrelevant material and the problem.

● Allow this thinking to generate new springboards or ideas.

If you think this sounds ridiculous, remember that judgement is suspended throughout this activity.

If you are still unsure, think about this. When doctors examined Einstein's brain after his death they discovered it had many more synapses than a normal brain. It could   conceivably make more connections faster than the average person. The suggestion is that this ability to make connections is how people innovate.

Another quote from Einstein:

   'You cannot solve a problem with the thinking that created it.'

Journey into Absurdity

Why use absurdity?

● To expand the range of possibilities when addressing a problem or opportunity.

● To increase potential for newness in the final ideas.

● To loosen the self-censor.

Characteristics of an absurd idea

Illegal	Impossible
Surprising	Fun
Unconventional	Illogical
Costs a lot	Once in a lifetime
Without conscience	Outrageous
Very risky	Shocking
Violates some basic laws of the universe, society or the company	Impractical

There are no rules about the right way to use absurd connections and ideas. They may have some element which directly addresses the problem — and they may have no connection at all!

Here are outline descriptions of some excursions, just to get you started.

Then go and invent some others for yourself. Some will work, others may not. It does not matter. There is no limit to how many you can use.

Imaging excursion

Additional ground rules

1. Keep the image visual
2. Keep it in one frame
3. Keep yourselves out

● The facilitator gives the group a word, ideally having some ambiguity, and not related to the issue.

● Do not write it down.

● Allow the group 5–10 seconds and then ask someone to describe their first thoughts as a picture, what they see, not as a radio play.

● Get participants to add in their first thoughts in turn.

● Ask someone to make something extraordinary happen.

● Have the group make private notes as they replay the image created.

● Use this material to trigger additional speculation.

Career excursion

● Give each group member a career or role.

● Ask participants to make notes about thoughts that arise as they think themselves into the role.

Either

● Use this material directly to trigger new springboards

or

● Have each participant talk to the group about their thoughts to trigger additional material and then get new springboards.

● A way to build on this if you want to have fun is to have the group play-act the roles when giving the springboards

Line drawing excursion

● Have each group member take a large marker pen and line them up in front of the flipchart pads.

● The first person draws a line, followed by everyone else in turn adding a line.

● Each additional line should touch the previous line in one place only, and not cross any other line, including itself.

● Continue this until you have had enough.

● Have the group focus on the pictures and use their thoughts to trigger more springboards.

Outside excursion

- Send the group outside and ask them to focus on something that intrigues or appeals to them.

- Make notes about it and share this material on returning to the room to use as new triggers.

- Alternatively, get participants to bring a range of objects back into the room and place them in a group in the middle as triggers.

- A high-tech build is to give everyone a Polaroid camera and put the results on a wall, using this as trigger material.

Analogy excursion

- Have the participants imagine becoming a part of an inanimate or live object. Describe to the group how it feels and the relationships with other objects.

- Use the material to trigger new springboards.

Example excursion

- Ask the problem owner to identify the essence of the need in order to make progress.

- Ask the group to give you examples of this need from two worlds unrelated to the problem.

- List examples on a flipchart.

- Ask the group to use the examples to trigger new springboards.

For example, if the problem owner is saying, 'my key need is to get people working together who are currently not able to,' we might suggest that it sounds like you are trying to create unlikely partnerships.

Therefore, get the group to list examples of unlikely partnerships in the worlds of 'nature' and 'theatre'. In nature, an example might be the birds that pick the crumbs out of the teeth of some animals.

So what are the attributes of this relationship and how can they be connected with the problem under discussion to give new perspectives to the thinking?

The case of the fired-up fireman

A group of consumers was involved in a difficult technical innovation session in the pharmaceutical industry. The group were looking for new applications for a very obscure breakthrough in biochemistry.

One of the group members was a fireman, who lacked any of the technical education and expertise of the client research team. He was wondering why he was there and initially felt very uncomfortable.

However, the fireman came up with a new and very exciting idea for using the product in personal healthcare for children.

The case of the need for speed

An invention group is trained to understand that implementation is the real test of effectiveness. An idea is a relatively small beginning. It is the continuing creative nourishment of the idea as it evolves that really makes the difference. One of the critical dimensions is time. It is critical to get things done without long waits.

An invention group in a building materials company demonstrated the kind of action orientation that makes for success. The group had developed a new concept for roofing that would allow a significant saving in roof construction. They needed a model to demonstrate it, and this required extensive work in a saw mill. They took their plans to a saw mill in the area and were told that because of a backlog of work, it would be a month before they could have the finished model.

They held a planning meeting and approached the general manager of the mill. After explaining their need for speed and presenting the manager with a case of whisky to show their good intentions, they got permission to approach the mill foreman.

They explained the problem to him and told him that it was worth a great deal of money to them to get the model fast. For example, if the usual charge for the work was $200, they would be happy to pay $600.

The mill foreman said, 'We have just added a late shift and we'll have your model in two days.'

Selection of Springboards

You can generate springboards for as long as you wish. It is a lot of fun.

Judging when it is appropriate to stop is a matter of experience. However, the following guidelines will give you a place to start.

The problem owner decides when to move on to the next stage of the process, and may care to be guided in this by the feelings of the group.

There is no right or wrong time. You are engaged in generating the creative fog, so it is not a rational process capable of objective judgement.

Selection is a key step in the process

and

needs to be given

a

**high** level of attention

Selection based on intrigue

Many brainstorming sessions end with someone deciding to review all the ideas listed, turning them into a list of **good** and **bad** ideas.

This is an objective and rational process.

The **good** ideas are the ones that can be made sense of, so the label good can be applied.

The **bad** ideas are the ones that nobody can make sense of. As such they contain all of the new thinking and are often rejected.

A rational selection is applied to the irrational process of **spring-boarding** and the result is that the very ideas that **might** lead to innovative possible solutions are rejected.

We could go along with the above process — but we would want to throw away the **good** ideas and work with the **bad**.

Our belief is that people are unable to use the **bad** ideas because they have no process for turning them into possible solutions.

We offer two key processes to allow you to use springboards:

● **selection**

and

● **idea development**

The problem owner selects *one* **springboard**, based on what he or she feels to be a high level of **intrigue**.

So what is this concept called **intrigue**?

**Seeing the light
at the end of the
tunnel**

**Looking into pitch
darkness**

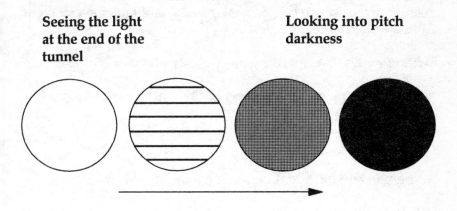

Increasing level of intrigue

Imagine a tunnel on the left where you can see the light at the end of the tunnel. You know where it goes. It takes you to a known destination. This means it is a feasible journey, boring and unlikely to take you somewhere new.

If you choose a **springboard** in this tunnel you are unlikely to innovate.

As the tunnels move to the right they become darker. On the right is a black hole that could lead somewhere exciting, or it may be a brick wall. You will never know unless you travel the path.

Springboards in this tunnel are **intriguing**. They are exciting because they go into the unknown. It is risky, and the journey lacks feasibility because you do not know yet where you are going.

This tunnel **may** lead you to new and innovative possible solutions.

Another way to conceptualize intrigue is to imagine a beach backed by limestone cliffs full of caves.

Think about when you were a child. Maybe you came across a shallow cave and you could squat inside it and imagine you were a shipwrecked sailor.

Exciting for a while, but the game quickly becomes boring.

Around the corner is a much deeper cave that disappears around a corner and into the dark.

This is exciting!

You step in and quickly it becomes dark and cold.

This is scary!

You step further in and can make out something in the back around the corner, a passage.

Does it lead to the pirates' treasure, or are you going to step off a cliff and fall into a deep hole?

This is intriguing.

Intrigue is a vital step in the creative problem-solving process. Give time to allow the problem owner to review the springboards and become intrigued. You have to play with the thoughts and let them develop. Intrigue sometimes just happens, and sometimes you need to let your mind mull things over for a while.

Idea Development

Selection gave you a way to make choices from springboards. If you have chosen something intriguing the chances are that it makes no sense in a rational world.

It is intriguing!

Idea development is the process that allows you to use the type of speculation generated during springboards and turn it into possible innovative solutions.

The role of the problem owner is to give direction to the group.

This is a key role at this point in the process. Unless the problem owner is able to give direction to the group, the group members will have no way to generate further ideas.

Without direction from the problem owner, the group will be left floundering in the creative fog with no way out.

Idea development is often tough, like swimming through treacle with your hands tied behind your back.

The key steps are:

● Work with one **springboard** at a time — you can always go back and try others later.

● The problem owner talks to the group about the intrigue, and the group uses **in/out listening** to trigger specific and actionable ideas that would deliver the intrigue.

Specific and actionable ideas use a headline format like:

What you do is...

This is different from wishing, which is speculative. You have expanded your thinking to the maximum width of the kite, made a selection, and now you are going to begin **gradually to introduce feasibility**.

1. The group generate a series of specific and actionable ideas, fewer of them than for springboards. The problem owner should join in and give ideas as well.

2. Stop after a while and invite the problem owner to consider the ideas to see if **one or more of them is beginning to suggest a concept or direction of thinking that could be pursued further**.

3. If not, continue to get more ideas. Use an **excursion** if you wish to keep the thinking open minded.

4. If yes, get the problem owner to use an **itemized response** to identify the pluses, and one major concern.

5. Collect ideas to address the concern and then go back to the problem owner and repeat the process from step 2.

6. Keep cycling through the process until you get to a solution, or decide it is going nowhere and try another springboard.

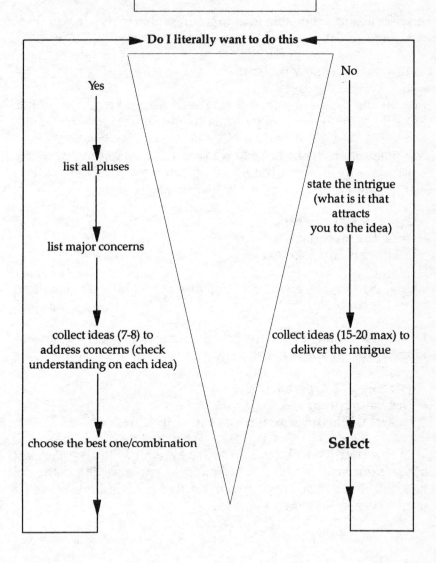

Selection

Do I literally want to do this

Yes

No

list all pluses

state the intrigue
(what is it that
attracts
you to the idea)

list major concerns

collect ideas (7-8) to
address concerns (check
understanding on each idea)

collect ideas (15-20 max) to
deliver the intrigue

choose the best one/combination

Select

Take the following example.

My problem is: **How to keep the office quieter**.

The springboard I have chosen is: **I wish you could stop James from talking so loudly**.

A specific and actionable idea to address this is: **What you do is cut his head off**.

This would solve my problem.

List all the pluses for this idea. There are many…for example: I like the speed and finality of this suggestion.

My major concern is: **how to do this without getting arrested**. I need a way to have the effect of cutting a head off without actually doing it. Give me some further ideas.

Put a muzzle on him.
Tape his mouth up.
Staple his lips together.

These are looking good, nothing illegal here and they will all solve the problem.

I like the muzzling of sound concept. My major concern is: **how to muzzle him in a less antisocial way**.

Put him in a separate office.
Use soundproof screens.
Install white noise generators tuned to James.

This is a contrived illustration to try and get a difficult concept across. You will see how a ludicrous suggestion like cutting a head off, treated positively using an **itemized response**, can be used to generate more feasible ideas.

Developmental Thinking Exercise

The purpose of this exercise is to practise the **Idea--Paraphrase--Itemized Response** sequence to develop from a starting idea to a course of action which is new, appealing and feasible, in the judgement of the problem owner.

To obtain maximum benefit from the exercise, keep strictly to the roles and follow the steps exactly.

PROBLEM OWNER (CLIENT)	HELPER (RESOURCE)
1. States task headline and gives background information. Why there is a problem/ opportunity for him/ her. What tried and thought of. His/her power and willingness to act. What would he/she wish for.	Listens for ideas, makes notes of thoughts triggered, without judging their relevance. **NO QUESTIONS!**
2. Listens to understand.	Offers ONE actionable idea that is likely to be NOVEL to problem owner.
3. Paraphrases the idea.	Checks that the paraphrase is accurate, clarifies if necessary.
4. Identifies all the good points of the idea. Then gives direction for next idea or improvement to the offered idea. "What I need now is a way to ..." (This can be either "a way to deal with the major negative in the first idea", or "a way to achieve the objectives with a different kind of idea"). Problem owner has choice of whether to develop an appealing idea, or ask for a replacement to an idea that is not appealing.	Listens for ideas. (Does not join in the evaluation.)

5. Helper offers new idea (or builds on original ideas) to meet the need expressed by problem owner, who processes the idea as in Steps 3 and 4.

   Continue in this sequence until the problem owner has a course of action which he judges to be new, appealing and feasible.

Next Steps

Finish with some next steps

otherwise

why bother to make the effort?

Ensure every action has

a name and

a time on it

The case of the one-sided jury

In a well-known graduate school of architecture, the Dean wanted to see whether innovation training would increase the effectiveness of his students in landscape architecture. He divided his class of 18 students into two teams of 9, making them as even in talent as he could. One team was trained in innovation skills, the other team went through the usual training in problem solving and invention.

Both teams were given the same several-acre site and asked to design the landscape around three buildings that were to be constructed.

It is the practice in such schools to invite several outside professionals to act as a 'jury' to evaluate the students' work. In this case, each team presented their final designs and the jury gave such one-sided approval to the innovation trained team that the other team protested the experiment would have an unfair and serious effect on their individual academic standings. The Dean assured them comparison would not be 'held against' them and they would get the training in the next semester.

Learning from Actual Experience

When you try out creative problem-solving meetings for yourself, notice how you feel, notice what you think about, notice how you behave during the different phases of the meeting.

Notice also how other people appear to respond or participate. The following checklist may be helpful.

Task headline

	Myself	Group members
Springboards		
Excursion		

	Myself	Group members
Selection		
Idea development		
Next steps		

Part Two
How Innovation Works

Introduction

This section of the not-a-book is a map of the territory of innovation. This section describes the territory in general terms. It should help you in recognizing things as you come across them in your journey through the territory. You can, of course, explore the territory without a map; the map is most useful when you take it with you on a journey into the territory; if you read the map without going on a journey you will learn little from the map.

As a starting point, the table below summarizes what is different in this territory from the landscape that you are familiar with in working in business.

Typical existing innovation systems	What we propose
Commercial innovation as a programmable, linear process	Commercial innovation as chaotic and unpredictable by its nature
Set success criteria at the outset; reject proposals that do not meet them	Search very widely; explore what is found from many perspectives
Set market impact goals; control at intermediate milestones	Look for and examine opportunities as they arise
Manage risks carefully to ensure project remains inside control limits	Climb one hill at a time; replan your route from the top of each hill
Create explanatory models to understand and predict the world	People interact directly with the world and follow their intuition
Rely on system to decide action, ensuring output matches criteria	Take personal control; choose outputs of intuitive appeal
People involved work with the system and depend on it	People learn from their experience, and are enabled to act directly

Managing the Process : 'Following the Star'

INNOVATION PROJECT STRUCTURES AND PROCESSES

In broad terms an innovation project is like any other project. It will have:

- a project team, with a project leader;
- a level of acceptance from the rest of the organization;
- some vision or goals for the end-state and what is to be achieved;
- a programme with phases or milestones that map out progress;
- a monitoring process, so that progress can be tracked on an ongoing basis.

Depending on the scale of the project, and the culture of the organization, these various things may be more or less explicit and formalized.

What differentiates an innovation project from other projects is that the vision/goal/end-state:

- is subject to radical revision during the project, in the light of progress;
- is defined very loosely.

An important consequence is that it can be very difficult to know where you are in relation to the ultimate end point — like pursuing the mirage of an oasis across the desert, or following a star to a distant, unknown destination.

Our diagram for the six-step structure of an innovation project is on the next page.

Map of the innovation process

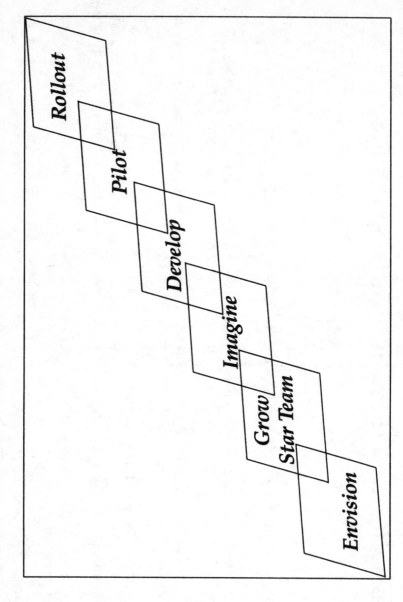

The whole innovation programme — and each of the six steps, and each moment of each step — contains the same progression. This progression is the map of the map and the steps of the steps. It moves from creation to implementation.

The map of the map and the steps of the steps

IMPLEMENTATION

- Structures and processes

- People and culture

- Exploring and experimenting

- Creating the climate

CREATION

The first activity within this framework is **creating the climate**.

In an early scene in the film *Crocodile Dundee* the hero is wrestling with a stuffed crocodile in a bar in the deep outback. This 'creates the climate' in a very clear way:

● It is symbolic — of the culture and the theme.

● It is a reflection of the main purpose, rather than part of it.

● It models kinds of behaviour that are going to be important, but it is not yet 'for real'.

● It invites other people to join in, in whatever way they may wish.

The next activity is **exploring and experimenting**:

● This is taking advantage of a more open climate to try out things that cannot be justified on a rational basis in advance. It involves using the 'ready/fire/aim' strategy of doing something and learning from the experience that underpins the innovative approach. It embodies the approach that is needed when you are venturing into new territory where the consequences of your actions are difficult or impossible to foresee.

The third activity is **connecting into the people and culture**:

● This is bringing these new experiments and experiences to the people in the group and the wider organization. It is followed by enabling people to build commitment to the new ideas through taking them on board and modifying them to better match the existing reality as it is perceived. This means building something new enough to be valuable while being capable of fitting into the stable parts of the context.

The last activity is **creating new structures and/or processes**:

- which will cement the new approaches into the broad organization that people recognize as 'their' company, overcoming the 'immune' response which can lead to rejection of the new.

Each step is expanded in the following set of six diagrams. Each diagram has within each programme step:

- at top left: actions for the **opening/creative** theme;
- at bottom right: actions for the **closure/implementation** theme.

What is important here is the alternance of opening and closing within each step. This is the cycle which keeps the project alive and healthy.

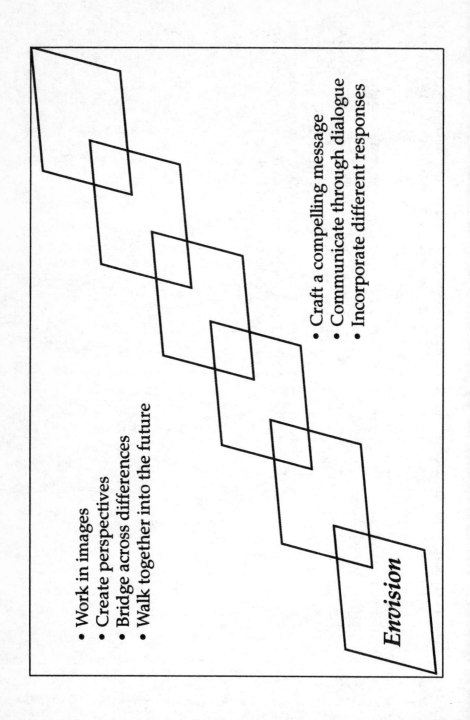

- Work in images
- Create perspectives
- Bridge across differences
- Walk together into the future

- Craft a compelling message
- Communicate through dialogue
- Incorporate different responses

Envision

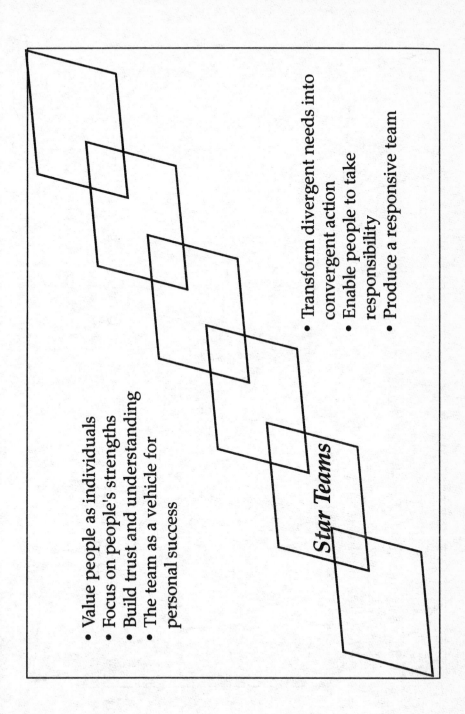

- Value people as individuals
- Focus on people's strengths
- Build trust and understanding
- The team as a vehicle for personal success

- Transform divergent needs into convergent action
- Enable people to take responsibility
- Produce a responsive team

Star Teams

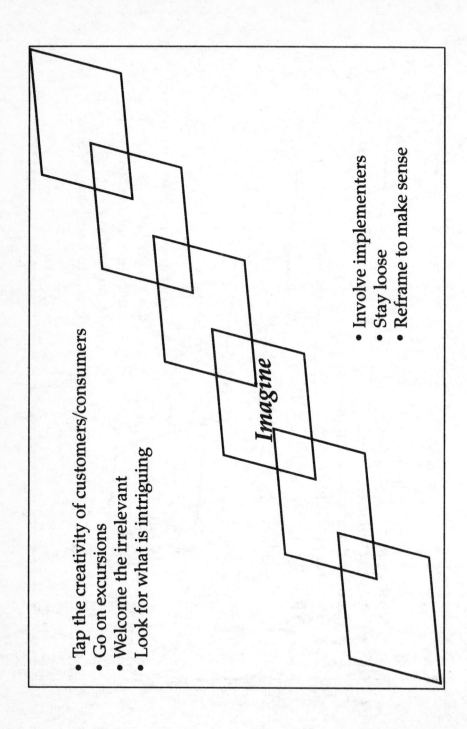

- Tap the creativity of customers/consumers
- Go on excursions
- Welcome the irrelevant
- Look for what is intriguing

Imagine

- Involve implementers
- Stay loose
- Reframe to make sense

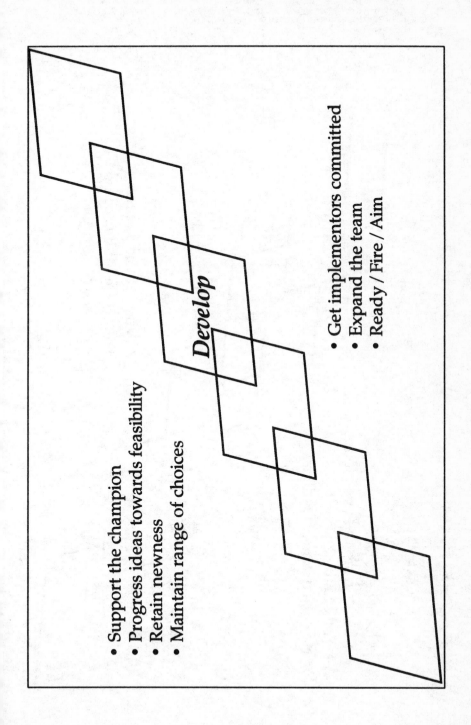

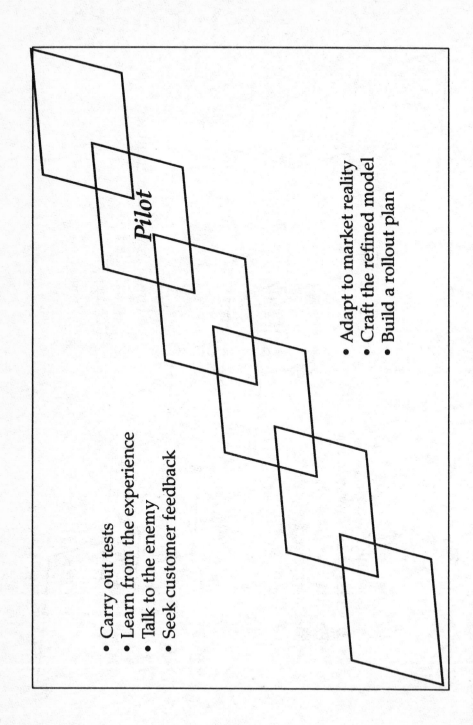

Pilot

- Carry out tests
- Learn from the experience
- Talk to the enemy
- Seek customer feedback

- Adapt to market reality
- Craft the refined model
- Build a rollout plan

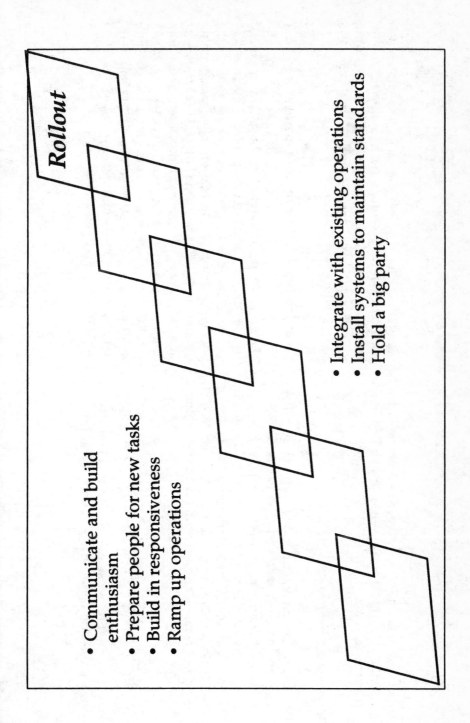

Rollout

- Communicate and build enthusiasm
- Prepare people for new tasks
- Build in responsiveness
- Ramp up operations
- Integrate with existing operations
- Install systems to maintain standards
- Hold a big party

MAINTAINING CONTROL

This is control in the same way that surfers have control when they ride a wave — it is a live and not a rigid process.

Organizing the project

Organizing an innovation project is much like organizing any other project. You need to decide who is involved, what the goals are, how long it should take, who needs the results. You need to know who should be involved outside the immediate project team, when and how often. You need to decide what the project team is authorized to do and what limits its authority has.

Get started: Ready/fire/aim

It is important to get started before you know what you are doing: that is the meaning of ready/fire/aim. This is the strategy for action when you do not know the consequences of the action you are going to take. **Innovation is all about doing something new and not knowing the consequences.**

Seeing in the dark: learn from experience

The art of seeing in the dark is learned from experience as you go along and interpreting the echoes that you send ahead of you. It is being always alert to the possibility that new information contains something different than what has gone before. In searching for something new, it is important to remember that **'knowing where you are going means going where you know'**. Each new experience offers the possibility of many different interpretations. It is important to be open to as many of these as possible when you are trying to interpret the experience.

Experience based control

In a conventional control system, you know how to act in the light of the feedback information: you know how to make a correction and get back on course. **In an innovation project, you cannot be sure of either the course or the meaning of the feedback information.** This makes it essential to use your own intuition as well as the intuition of those around you in deciding what to do. Using a reporting system (based on 'evidence') shuts out the bulk of the information available because that information is unexpected. Only by personal experience of what is happening is it possible to identify the key information and the insights that it brings.

Managing process not content

Managing process means managing how things are done rather than what is done. The 'tools' section in Part One reviews a number of our techniques for managing innovation processes.

Paying attention to these process management techniques can ensure that the innovation process moves forwards even when you don't know what will emerge from it. This avoids getting bogged down by the uncertainty around the content.

Transferring the results

In order for the results of the process to emerge as innovation, they have eventually to be transferred into the body of the organization as a new product, a new way of working, or whatever. In general, the people who finally receive the results have been involved to a very limited extent, if at all, in their conception. Making the transfer process effective demands paying close attention to when and where the recipients of the results get involved. In general, the earlier they are involved, the greater will be their commitment to the final outcome and the easier the transfer of results will become.

THINKING AND ACTION

The diagram below is constructed with two axes:

● Thinking. This runs from ideas — vague, nebulous, of uncertain origin, to information — hard, testable facts.

● Action. This runs from planning your work and working your plan, to responding instantly — in the blink of an eye.

Thinking and action

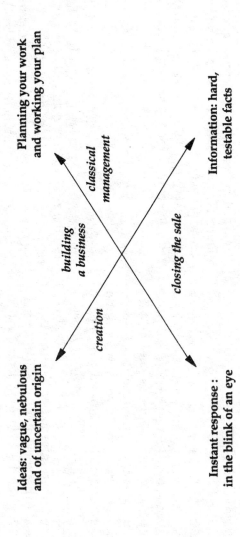

Planning your work
and working your plan

classical
management

building
a business

closing the sale

creation

Ideas: vague, nebulous
and of uncertain origin

Information: hard,
testable facts

Instant response :
in the blink of an eye

This is a book (despite what we said earlier about it being not-a-book). Books contain ideas and information; this is generally what people value them for. They can also, for example, serve to hold up a table leg which is shorter than the others, provide fuel when burnt on the fire, act as a missile in a domestic dispute and so forth.

Ideas and information can be seen as the ends of a scale, on which there are also various intermediate points. Things that lie at the **ideas** end of the scale will typically:

● come to mind without being called for, and may or may not seem relevant to the needs of the moment

● be rather vague, imprecise and hard to pin down exactly

● arrive intuitively, without their origin being immediately apparent.

At the other end of the scale lies **hard information**. This is typically:

● an accurate picture of an external reality — like a telephone number

● provable or testable in the real world

● something that you have deliberately called for, because you need it for some purpose: it is more a tool than an end in itself.

In between these two ends of the scale lie such things as:

● opinions: the holder often takes these as facts, believing them proved by their own experience

● theories: usually testable, but more like useful simplifications of reality than reality itself.

In the context of this book, ideas are important because they are a kind of raw material for the innovation process.

No matter how well organized and thought through your innovation process, the output will be thin stuff unless adequate ideas are fed in.

For large and sophisticated companies this is often the key barrier to successful innovation.

Part One offers a wide range of techniques for idea generation. Here, we want to consider ideas as stuff: what are the characteristics of this material that is apparently so important to successful innovation. People do not generally make pillows out of brick or saucepans out of plywood: what can and what cannot be made out of ideas? Ideas:

- are constantly around, like air

- are open and without boundaries rather than closed

- have a quality of vagueness and incompleteness

- are unstable and spontaneously change and transmute into other ideas.

They are a beginning, a medium for suggesting:

● other ideas so that something more detailed and complete can be built

● directions, possible ways of going further, avoidance of remaining stuck

● the expression of wishes and hopes of how things might become in the future

● solutions to problems through metaphoric or poetic means

● a partial answer, a piece of a larger solution or way forward.

The content of the ideas can be:

● inspired, coming from intuition rather than logic

● something entirely new, that never existed before

● something you did not know that you already knew

During the years you spent being educated from age five or so onwards, one of the things you learned a lot about was evaluation. The evaluation process was framed in terms of comparisons:

● a score out of ten, where ten is perfect

● a rank order in your class, where first is best

● an exam result, where less than x per cent is a failure.

This exposure conditions you to accept the importance and appropriateness of comparative judgements, where things are placed on a scale of right/wrong or true/false — in all situations. If the quality of the thing lies in its uniqueness — as with human beings, or emotional or physical experiences — then comparative evaluation of the conventional type has no meaning. Ideas, as they arise, are of this kind.

What is vitally important about ideas (i.e. this end of the ideas/information scale) is that there is: **no value in applying comparative right/wrong, true/false judgements to them.**

In relation to ideas, what you learned about evaluation is bullshit. As you move towards the **hard information** end of the scale, so conventional evaluation becomes more and more appropriate. In order to know whether the conventional evaluation process is appropriate, you have to be aware of what stuff you are dealing with.

Interactions between people often become disputes when there is a misunderstanding about the nature of what is under discussion: for example, 'I think we turn left here.' Did the speaker intend:

● to offer an idea
  – just one possibility among many?
  – should we put forward some other possibilities before selecting which one to go for?

● to give an opinion
  – that they believe this will be better than other possible alternatives?
  – should we find out the basis for this opinion?

● to provide factual information
  – we have in fact turned left here on previous occasions?
  – should we try to check the truth of the statement?

The response depends to a large degree on the respondent's understanding of the class of which the statement is a member. This exists at a different (meta) level from the explicit information in the statement.

Awareness of this meta level and responsiveness to it is what we call process. Some of our process management tools and concepts are set out in Part One. We see managing process in an explicit way as the key to success in innovation, where the scope for ambiguity and confusion is high.

Managing yourself: 'becoming the master of two worlds'

THE HERO'S JOURNEY

Many of the myth systems of different people around the world include examples of **the hero's journey**. A modern example is *The Wizard of Oz*. These myths around the hero or heroine and their journeys have a number of common characteristics:

- **heroes** are fairly ordinary people: they have their share, but not more, of courage, strength, persistence and so forth;

- they set off on their journeys without clearly knowing why, driven by an internal force they do not fully understand;

- their journeys take them away from their **home ground**, their familiar and comfortable surroundings, into unknown territory;

- the unknown territory contains various **ordeals** that they have to pass, from which they learn and develop at a personal level;

- they find eventually a **treasure** that they wish to bring back with them. The treasure may have material or more spiritual qualities;

- on their return to the home ground, people find it hard to accept them back. They have developed and changed, and have grown to value the treasure highly. Others may find it hard to see its value at first sight.

In the 1970s and 1980s people in large businesses used **decision-support systems**. These were intended to aid senior executives in complex decision making. They were predicated on various assumptions which are often partly true, including:

● people prefer to believe that the best course of action can be discovered by analysing the data rather than taking responsibility for decisions based on judgement;

● causality that operated in the past will continue to apply, so mathematical models built to fit what has happened in the past have value as predictors of the future;

● you already know more than you recognize, and tapping this hidden knowledge will improve your decisions;

● having a rational justification for your proposed actions is almost as good as being right.

Every project that brings real innovation can be seen as a **hero's journey**. The hero or heroine may be an individual, different individuals at different moments, or a team.

The key business issue in such projects is how to reconcile:

● the lack of precision in the forward plan, when you do not have:

– a thought-through rationale
– knowledge of the **treasure** that will be found at the end of the journey
– knowledge of the steps, **ordeals** that the journey will entail, or what it will take to succeed;

● the need to maintain control over utilization of resources, payback, return on investment.

We illustrate the applicability of these kinds of assumptions with the **cycling worlds** diagram (see page 30). This describes the business world in terms of two cycles:

● the world of routine, of ordinary day-to-day activity, which occupies the bulk of our working time no matter what our job;

● the world of innovation, of development, of creating new ways of doing things that by definition are less familiar and require a degree of experimentation and trial and error.

The more newness there is in the situation, the less is it possible to apply rational methods based on what has applied in the past, the **decision-support systems** approach.

A well-known example of this kind of situation is provided by mergers between different companies to create a new entity.

The only sure thing about such a merger is that it is unique, and the outcome is not predictable from data on previous mergers or other events. However, despite the fact that this is both obvious and well known, people generally proceed as though it were not true.

ALTERNANCE

Typical management processes are based around the assumption that things are going to go on broadly as they went on before. There may be minor changes, but it is not a question of going and then coming back all the time.

Watching people playing polo while riding motorcycles illustrates the advantages of horses for this game. Horses are designed to be effective at changing direction and altering speed very suddenly. Motorbikes are not designed for that. They are good at going very fast — they go faster than horses in a straight line or round a steady curve — but if you want to get quickly to somewhere and you don't know where until the last moment, then use a horse.

Innovation is a question of going and then coming back all the time — it is that kind of process, a kind that involves constantly changing direction and going back on your tracks. When you get there, you will know where it was you were going, but you don't know that beforehand. Before you have arrived at the destination you do not know whether the direction that you are going in is the right one or not.

What is the sound of one hand clapping? It is like applying a conventional management process to the management of innovation.

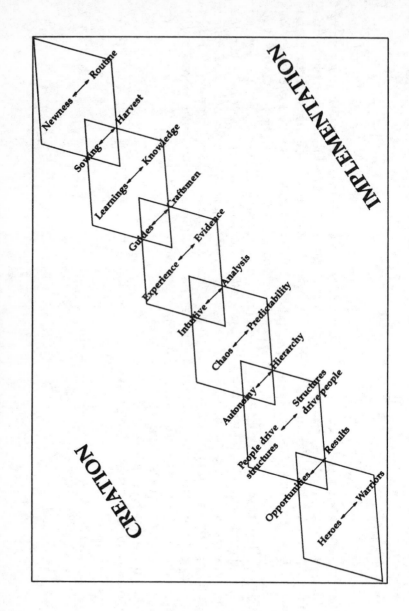

One way to think about this is imagining that you can see the world as real and its reflection in a mirror as an illusion, but at any one moment you don't know which is real or which is the illusion. When the wind raises a cloud of dust, you see the dust but you cannot see the wind which carries it. Yet it is the wind which is the reality behind the dust cloud.

For example, a map is a reflection of the real territory. The map and the territory are not the same. When you have the map in your hand the map is real, while the territory is an illusion, out beyond you somewhere stretching into the distance. When you are walking up the mountain the mountain is real, the map is a piece of paper folded in your backpack. Both the map and the territory are real and both are illusion. They are reflections of each other in the mirror. It is this 'mirror' effect which enables you to make progress. From the map, you can recognize the territory — and from the territory you can recognize the map.

Applying alternance is learning to move from one side of the mirror to the other, mastering the worlds of reality and illusion at the same time in parallel with each other. In this way you can be sure that when you arrive at the destination you will be in touch with reality: because you are constantly in touch with it, and also constantly out of touch with it.

Alternance is the process of constantly moving from one state to the other, putting your weight on one foot and then on the other, breathing in and then breathing out. Thinking and action have the same kind of relation to each other: thinking without action achieves nothing, action without thinking goes backwards as easily as it goes forwards.

Alternance:
Stepping through the Mirror

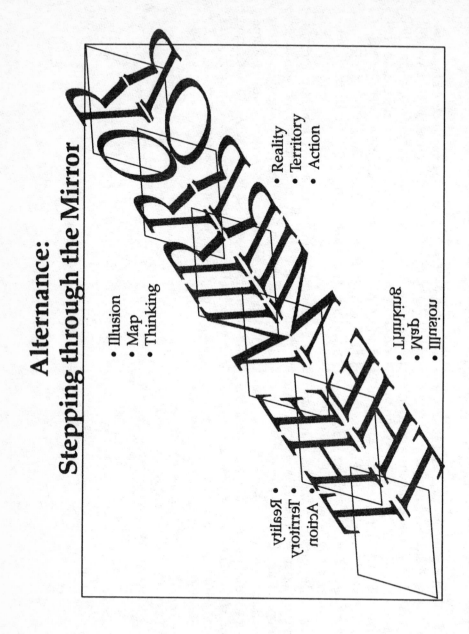

- Illusion
- Map
- Thinking

- Reality
- Territory
- Action

The opportunity for making progress under these conditions is normally in the moments of transition. The moment of power in walking is when you shift your balance and spring off again from the other foot.

The diagram on page 128 shows transitions as between creation and implementation, the two opposite poles of our innovation map. In order to innovate we need to be consistently alternating between creation and implementation in big steps as in small ones. If we stay with implementation ('what is practical') then we shall not do anything new. If we stay with creation we shall float in the clouds and not bring something new into reality. We need to step first with the left leg and then with the right leg: we can't make all our left steps first, and then all our right steps.

Each transition contains a paradox. One cannot simultaneously:

● be both chaotic and predictable

● rely both on evidence and experience

● focus one's attention on learning and on what one already knows.

We see the secret as being able to alternate between these different states and to do this very fast, never knowing beforehand which is the appropriate state for the new moment. This seems to connect with Heisenberg's uncertainty principle: the more you know about where you are the less you know about where you are going.

These are the characteristics that make the process so difficult to manage in a classical sense.

LOOKING BEYOND THE HORIZON

Consider how it is for an ant. A rut looks about like the Grand Canyon does to us. As he looks up he can see the sky above, while the edges of the rut cut off the lower part of the sky and form his horizon. For each of us, the horizon is the edge of the rut we are in at the moment. Our rut occupies a large part of our time and attention and forms the main focus for our day-to-day lives.

What do we like about our rut?

● It provides that minimum of stability in our lives, enough points of reference which seem fixed, which we need to survive at all.

● It defines our comfort zone, the area of the world we know and are familiar with, so the frightening unknown is shut away on the outside.

● It provides justification for accepting things as they are, not being locked in a hopeless struggle against external powers as we try to shape the world to our own desires.

Most of us have personal experience of being in a rut: the symptoms can include:

● the weight of tasks pressing in, that seem not as productive as once they may have been;

● the sense of running to stay in the same place, making effort but no progress;

● applying a recipe we have used before successfully, and observing that it does not work on this occasion — and not knowing why;

● an impression of being trapped by circumstances that we cannot control.

An organization, or an individual, who is going to be successful in innovation requires:

● awareness that the rut is there, restricting the view even when we do not notice it directly;

● recognition that staying in the rut or going beyond it is a choice we are free to make: it is our responsibility to decide when to make a new choice;

● acceptance that there is no way to know for certain which is the better choice at any one moment; and that different people will choose differently.

This book does not, and cannot, decide for you what you should do in your specific situation.

What it does provide is help in:

● examining the possible consequences before you opt to climb out of your rut;

● offer reflections and a sounding board for you once you climb out and start your innovation journey.

Innovation means choosing to look beyond the horizon. This is the **hero's journey**. The characteristics of the hero, and the other members of the cast that make up your personality, are described in the next section of this part, which deals with being a hero and not being a hero. Some of the tools that will be useful in the encounters on the way are set out in Part One of the not-a-book.

Managing others: 'directing the cast'

HOW DIFFERENT PEOPLE WORK DIFFERENTLY

There are various systems for describing the different roles or personalities that people demonstrate in their interactions as a team. We use the basic Jungian model, and we have deliberately chosen a new set of names which:

● are a metaphor distanced from current business practice;

● are relevant and appropriate to the tasks of innovation;

● we have found helpful with business clients.

The names are roles at the court in a mediaeval kingdom. We refer to the whole set of roles as the **cast**. This can be a set of different individuals, or else different aspects of a few (or a single) individual.

Everyone is all of these roles — for each of us which role is at the forefront depends on:

● personal predisposition

● the moment

● the mood

● the context.

The Kingdom

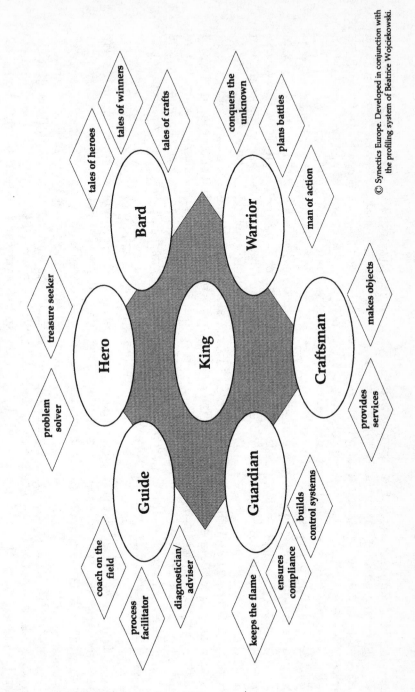

tales of heroes
tales of winners
tales of crafts
conquers the unknown
plans battles
man of action

Bard
Warrior

treasure seeker

Hero
King
Craftsman

makes objects

problem solver

provides services

coach on the field

Guide
Guardian

builds control systems

process facilitator
diagnostician/ adviser
keeps the flame
ensures compliance

The kingdom diagram describes how people act: typically and from moment to moment. People have a natural ability in some roles rather than others: in these roles they are at their best, fully themselves and fully effective. However, with enough effort each of us can play any of the roles when we choose. We need to learn to acknowledge the value of each role, because then we can acknowledge the value of our colleagues who play roles normally different from our own. The diagram can be used to describe a team with different individuals playing different roles. It can also describe a single individual who plays different roles at different times.

The diagram uses masculine terms such as king, man of action and craftsman — this is not intended to exclude women, but is merely for the sake of simplicity.

The people who find it easiest to understand each other are the ones adjacent to each other on the diagram: those who find it most difficult are on opposite sides of it.

For example, warriors are focused on organizing and making things happen. They make plans, assign roles and lead the action. They drive people along.

Guides (on the opposite side from warriors) try and help people do what they want to do for themselves. They offer advice, imagine options, suggest alternative ways of doing things and help people improve their performance.

In this approach the drive for improvement comes from the people themselves, not from the guide. This is very different from the approach of the warrior. There are moments when the leadership of the warrior is entirely appropriate: telling people what to do, not allowing discussion or dissent but ensuring everyone is getting on with it and going in the same direction. This is needed when time is short, when a systematic decision has to be made because the situation demands decision. This is the moment for the warrior.

The guide is about helping people decide for themselves what they will do, think about the various different possibilities, check what they really want to do by looking inside themselves, allowing lots of different views and opinions to exist at the same time. The leadership of the guide is appropriate when people need to develop personal commitment to the action and take personal responsibility for their own contribution to it and for its overall success. This is needed when the situation is a new one, there is a lot of confusion and no existing model.

Warriors provide directive leadership and welcome it; guides don't provide directive leadership and reject it when it is offered. Business provides constant tension between the need to decide what action to take now and the need to get people committed, give them time to think about the situation, help them understand. Those two different kinds of people find it difficult to hear each other's points of view. Both need to recognize that the other has value, that there are times when the other's view and approach are the more appropriate. This is hard to hear in the moment of battle.

In very general terms, those personalities near the top of the diagram prefer to spend their time in exploring new things, trying things out, looking at options, ranging widely. As we go towards the bottom, so the personalities give more attention to becoming focused, being action oriented, getting results rather than exploring possibilities. The cycle for an innovation process starts approximately from the personalities near the top of the diagram and progresses down to those near the bottom. It may all be inside the head of one person, but the way of looking at things and the decision process still moves down the diagram as we go from conception and creation towards implementation and completion.

Businesses tend to be focused on getting results and to reward people who are warriors, or behave like warriors, the people who 'get results'. Warriors are good for organizing systematic action, when the situation and the goals are clear. This means that people in business tend to think that they ought to be warriors — and some of them are. It is also important to remember that a business requires all kinds of people — a complete set of personalities — if it is to be successful in the long term. It also requires some of the qualities of the king. The king, at the centre of the diamond, is a different kind of individual, one not about action, but about being: about ends rather than means.

Successful innovation needs the role directing the action to move through a cycle from one member of the **cast** to the next.

Directing role	State of mind/attitude	Example
1 Craftsman	'I've used this model consistently.' 'If it ain't broke, don't fix it.'	'The wheel is a real breakthrough.' 'Carts are very successful — they have transformed our lives.'
3 Hero	'I have a vision of how it might be.'	'I want to fly in the air like a bird.'
4 Warrior	'Here are the goals we have to achieve.'	'We must design a wing that works.'
5 Guide	'Let's invent a way to reach the goals.'	'What's like a wing? Maybe a kite.'
6 Bard	'Hey, everybody — do I have news for you!'	'The Wright brothers have got it into the air.'
1 Craftsman	'The new model is great, now we've grasped it.'	'Only a biplane gives enough lift.'
2 Guardian	'Let's make sure we keep a firm hold of it.'	'Comet airliners broke the golden rule.'

We suggest you think of an innovation project that you have carried out on your own (either at work or in your private life.) Using the six roles in the order given above, identify eight phases in your project that correspond approximately to the eight steps listed, and fill in the table below (using key words).

Directing role	Your own state of mind/attitude	Tasks/what you worked on
1 Craftsman		
2 Guardian		
3 Hero		
4 Warrior		
5 Guide		
6 Bard		
1 Craftsman		
2 Guardian		

Most people — probably you included — find that, in thinking this exercise through:

● the different aspects/roles worked fairly well together, and got a result;

● some of the roles took a lot more of your time, attention and interest than others.

This exercise illustrates some important points about the process of innovation:

● Success demands the collaboration of a number of different members of the cast.

● These members of the cast have different priorities when it comes to action.

● The appropriate action priorities change as the innovation process proceeds — there is not one right set of priorities that applies all the time.

● These different priorities often lead to conflict when the personalities concerned are different individuals, rather than (as in the exercise) different aspects of the same person.

People tend to see the world from the particular standpoint of one of the characters; this standpoint brings with it particular priorities for action, which are different for different characters.

The following tables illustrate how expressing some of these different priorities appears to the various protagonists. Again, the male pronoun is used throughout merely for the sake of simplicity.

What the Hero says/does	Why	How it can by seen by
They say 'one cannot find it'. That which cannot be found — that is what I want. (Sufi proverb)	'Life is either a daring adventure or nothing.' (Helen Keller)	**Bard**: He generates lots of ideas and enthuses people for the moment, but he makes no effort to really persuade them.
Tomorrow is today's dream. When you work, you fulfill a part of earth's dream.' (Khalil Gibran)	I am driven by my imagination, my creative insight and my very personal vision of the world.	**Warrior**: He paints this wonderful vision but he does not have a way to make it happen.
I often work on several projects at the same time, and concentrate where my enthusiasm is at the moment.	'Nothing is more dangerous than an idea when it is the only idea you have.' (E. Chartier)	**Craftsman**: He begins lots of things but he never finishes any of them. He is not professional, and does not value our skills and experience.
I am very good at problem solving, particularly in new, chaotic or complex situations.	Crisis situations are opportunities to question our current approaches and to evolve, innovate and change.	**Guardian**: He is always questioning things that are well established and reliable; he does not respect our methods and procedures.
I need to work independently and alone, and I ignore timetables. I don't want inputs from other people.	Being independent and listening to my own inspiration and insight is what drives me.	**Guide**: He brings new perspectives and change and development, but he is no teamworker.

What the Bard says/does	Why	How it can be seen by
I often have a sense of what people should do differently.	I have perspective on things, and more of a sense of what will succeed than people on the inside, immersed in the work.	**Warrior**: We need you to be doing something useful, not just telling people about it.
Hey! My idea is brilliant — it will change your life!	I have a good overview, but I rely on other people who are specialists to deliver the results. I don't work at the detail level.	**Craftsman**: He sells the moon painted blue and then I am supposed to deliver it: my job is keeping his promises.
I go with what seems right at the time. It may not work, but if so, I'll try something else.	Take advantage of every opportunity — you can never be sure beforehand which are going to be the winners.	**Guardian**: He is an opportunist. He is not reliable because he does not follow the proper procedures.
Do it this way — this is a valuable new approach that will bring you many benefits.	I am excited to have found something really new and different and I need to tell you about it.	**Guide**: People need to discover for themselves that it will be right for them. Telling them just gets in their way.
The idea has some potential, but it needs to be reshaped.	First of all, we need to think about who is going to buy it. It only has value if someone else is going to pay money for it.	**Hero**: He has stolen my idea and bastardized it — I don't think he really appreciated the full value of it.

What the Warrior says/does	Why	How it can be seen by
We need to get some decisions made quickly and build a plan, so we can get on with things.	If I don't take charge, people will never get started — they will just talk about it.	**Craftsman**: He makes all these decisions, but he doesn't take account of the time it needs to do it properly.
Once we have a clear objective we need to move quickly, without planning down to the last detail.	We need to move quickly to seize the opportunity; we can make adjustments only once we have got something started.	**Guardian**: It's very dangerous to start a course of action without fully knowing the consequences.
As soon as I see the course of action we have to follow to reach our objectives, we must push ahead immediately.	The priority here is putting the plan into action, pushing aside the obstacles that people raise so as to maintain progress.	**Guide**: He acts like a robot, not thinking about human implications of his decisions.
I set the goals and a realistic framework for people to follow, so we can be sure it's achievable.	We need to be sure we get concrete results out of this approach.	**Hero**: He restricts the possibilities with his particular vision of what is practical, so the creative opportunities are lost.
We need to know where we are going so as to be sure we are all going in the same direction.	Our efforts need to be coordinated so as to ensure we get good results.	**Bard**: Why does everything have to be so organized and systematic — the result is that we are not flexible enough to grasp opportunities when they arise.

What the Craftsman says/does	Why	How it can be seen by
What is right is obvious to me, although I may not be able to explain it. I want to do it in my own way.	I am a master of the task, with a lot of experience, and I know how to do it.	**Guardian**: Work needs to be systematized and codified: if it is not measurable, it is not manageable.
I have a good way of doing things which is reliable and has always produced good results for me.	I am sure of the quality of the results that my method will bring.	**Guide**: He finds it difficult to recognize when he needs to change, so it is difficult for me to help him.
We take pride in doing things the traditional way: people buy our products because they know what they will get.	The traditional way of doing things is better because it has been perfected through many years of experience.	**Hero**: His view of the world is firmly fixed in tradition and in the past: when things change he is lost.
I want to make sure the client gets exactly what they expect.	Our reputation depends on meeting the client's expectations precisely.	**Bard**: It's not enough — clients don't know all the things they need, and it's important for us to come up with new ideas and stay ahead of the market.
I need to go it my own way and at my own pace, and get it finished before I start something else.	I have to be sure that I know how to finish the thing before I start it.	**Warrior**: I get very impatient with this need to have all the details nailed down before we even start — it wastes a lot of time.

What the Guardian says/does	Why	How it can be seen by
This process/function has gone off the rails and it needs to be rectified. We have to remain credible with the clients.	The organization as a whole needs to be kept within the rules, so that it can be accepted by other organizations.	**Guide**: There are always exceptions and a need for human judgement. It is not believable that the rules will be right in every case.
We need to validate the ideas at a practical level before looking at their creative potential.	It proves that the thing has a value and is worth using and taking seriously.	**Hero**: This way of thinking doesn't allow anything new and so it kills innovation.
We need to deal with hard facts and hard evidence when assessing things, so as to avoid errors. We don't want to jump into something that has not been thoroughly tested.	It is important not to make costly mistakes.	**Bard**: This way of thinking means you will never be ahead of the competition — your competitors will take all the market before you are ready to move.
We need to be totally sure that the new approach will work, before we try it.	Safety is paramount — there is absolutely no room for mistakes in our business.	**Warrior**: He will never decide anything on his own, because he always needs more reassurance that it is the right decision.
We need to have the standards and procedures stated very clearly and explicitly, so that people can follow them easily.	We have to ensure that the know-how and skills we use are preserved and that everyone applies them correctly.	**Craftsman**: I know how to do things, and I like to do them in my own way, using my experience. He imposes procedures that get in the way rather than helping.

What the Guide says/does	Why	How it can be seen by
The best ideas for the client are the ones they generate themselves.	Clients know better than I do what they need, what kind of thing would make them enthusiastic.	**Hero:** He is a good support and he has lots of ideas, but he does not put them forward.
It is important to listen to clients' needs and leave things open until we find a solution that will be satisfactory for the client.	Selling is facilitating the client's decision-making processes, not persuading them to buy a ready-made solution. If what they buy is not exactly what they want, I will lose their trust.	**Bard:** He does not push hard enough to get the sale. He goes into the meeting without being determined enough to get a close. He does not do everything to ensure he gets the sale.
It is important to listen carefully to people's ideas, needs and concerns and build on their views and suggestions. The business results will depend on their satisfaction.	They are the ones who know the tasks from inside, therefore they must be consulted. If their views and suggestions are taken into consideration, they will be more committed.	**Warrior:** I get things clear and straightforward, and along he comes splitting hairs and making it complicated again. People have to fall in line with the company's goals.
I help people to invent new ways of working and try out new things so that they can choose what is best for themselves.	Everywhere I see people working like crazy and finding that life gets ever tougher.	**Craftsman:** He listens to me when I need to talk, but when it comes to doing things, why doesn't he use the proper methods?
There are always many possibilities for action and ways of doing things. I encourage people to be open minded and avoid making judgements.	The way to success is keeping options open as long as possible.	**Guardian:** He is often nebulous and does not see it as important to follow our existing procedures.

ENABLING DIFFERENT PEOPLE TO COLLABORATE: BUILDING ON STRENGTHS

This is about how people working together can grow into a team, in which each of them is a star. This is an image of a team where **people do what they are personally best at**. They are by no means interchangeable, each of them has their own strengths, and the team is built around those strengths. We believe effective teams are focused around people's strengths and provide a way for people to work with their strengths. They are not a device for helping people to overcome their weaknesses. The aim of the team is for people to stand out as a result of deploying their strengths, so that each individual (and other people) knows and can see how they have contributed their special strengths to the success of the team. So teams are ways to make you really different, not to make you the same as the others.

The diagram overleaf shows the underlying process for building a team. The process operates in two cycles, the first addressing the individuals in the team and the second the team as a whole. Each cycle has three stages, and is represented as a triangle. The principle of alternance applies here as before: the cycles may take many months to complete — or just a few seconds.

The process starts:

● from the top of the diagram

● with focus on individuals.

It moves around the inner triangle, to a completion for individuals, and then around the outer triangle, to a completion for the team.

The first phase is people focusing on their own strengths and taking opportunities to apply what they already know. The reality is, of course, that none of us can do more than apply what we already know. If we learn things, then next time we can apply new things, but in the moment we can only apply what we know now. Applying what we already know, undertaking that action, causes consequences and we can observe the consequences of our actions. The next phase is to understand those consequences — to learn from that experience.

Star teams

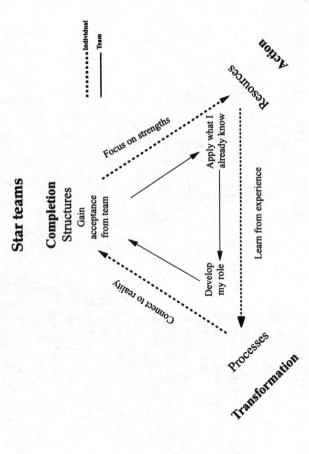

people feel there is a need for that role. The process here is identifying a role in my current situation, that I can fill effectively and that is also needed.

Once the people in the team have explored their roles and gained broad acceptance from others in the team about what those roles are, it is then possible for the team to start to work on what it can do as a collective. Now we know a lot about the strengths of the team and the things that particularly differentiate it. Again, watching the team in action helps us to understand what the team can do and what are the consequences of the action that it takes.

The team as a group needs to learn from experience of watching themselves in action. Each individual can learn about their own role, and there is also learning to do about the team as a whole, how can it best act in the situation in which it finds itself. This leads to thinking about how to transform the team into the most effective group or actor on the scene, identifying what other processes the team needs to be paying attention to, because those processes are the ones that best translate its own best capabilities into success. Having identified some new processes, then it is up to the team to try those processes out and see how they in fact correspond with its reality. As

This means understanding what it is that as an individual I specifically, uniquely, bring to my role in the situation. I need to understand that, so that in future I can do more of the thing that I am particularly good at. In looking at my experience, then, I need to understand where I did things that really counted, what those were and what kind of role that implies for me in the future. These are steps which can progressively lead to a transformation of how I do things, how I see myself, how others see me. This transformation leads me to be more and more confident in my strengths and to deploy them more and more effectively, to understand better and better my own reality.

The next stage for the individual, having gained some understanding around that potential transformation, is to identify how that connects into the reality of the situation in which they find themselves. The first stage is to check whether other people have something of the same experience of the reality. In order to be effective in my chosen role, others need to understand that role and to recognize that I can indeed play it effectively. I need to look at whether that is happening and, if it is happening, how well it is going. I need to understand how much other

It is possible to use this approach as a basis for a two- or three-day seminar to help with growing the team. It is also possible to use it all the time. The model does not have time dimensions on it. It is possible to go round that cycle in a few minutes or a year, but going round the cycle each time enhances the capability of the team and the satisfaction and the capability of the individuals within it.

understanding of the team's processes improves, so it is necessary progressively to put structures in place that enable the team to use those processes routinely without having to reinvent them or rediscover them each time. This brings us to a completion point where both the team and the individuals within it are all acting to the best of their ability — as stars — and are doing superbly well the things that they are best at.

What to do next

We have described the map of the innovation territory and offered some tools. So what is to be done with all this — what should you do now?

There are three areas for action. The first is to invest in people, invest in yourself and invest in others. Create the capacity for innovation, give people the opportunity to try it, encourage them, build relationships with them and between them, enable them to communicate about what they are doing and what they are learning. The second phase is around acquiring practical tools, which is what Part One of the book is designed to help you with. Knowing what to do is no help if you do not have the tools to actually do it — and having the tools is no help if you do not know what to do.

The third thing to do is build an innovation programme. Use the map that has been described in this part of the book, apply the tools, control the results from being involved through experience rather than through evidence and reporting. Stay personally connected to the innovation programme and it will succeed. Good luck!

Part Three
The Author is You

This section of the book poses a series of questions to you, the reader.

These are designed to get you thinking about how you behave to other people, and how other people behave towards you.

The thinking you record on these pages is your personal contribution to realizing your potential to be creative and innovative.

There are 100 ways of using this section. What is important is that you use it to connect to your actual experience. You could use it as a diary and make diary entries, you could take each experience and make notes when it happens for you. Any way you find helpful is fine.

The toolkit section at the other end of this not-a-book will give you some ways to experiment with behaviours positively, constructively and supportively, for creativity and innovation.

You may choose to use this section of the book first in order to explore the issues around innovation and creativity for yourself, or you may want to read the book and then use this section to exercise your new experiences of the world of innovation.

Either way is OK.

You choose.

There are no correct answers.

Creativity

is

like

sex

You can

read about it

You can

attend a lecture

and you will have to try it

to learn about
what it is really like

The meaning of any communication or interaction is the response that you get.

Sometimes the response will be the intended one, predictable, and the 'right' one.

Sometimes the response will be a surprise, not at all what you intended. This response may be useful and positive, at other times it will be very unhelpful.

The questions that you are asked to address have no right answers, they are your experiences of the different territories you will explore.

In generating a climate where innovation is possible, the opportunity is to get the most potential from any communication or interaction.

The range of questions is designed to help you explore the areas of communication and interaction that our experience suggests are important if you want to be an innovator.

Have fun!

To begin with, think about yourself.

In a creative thinking session, to what part of the meeting do you contribute most effectively, in your opinion?

What is your most valuable contribution?

What is happening when you are at your most creative?

What are you thinking about at this time?

How are you feeling at this time?

How are you behaving at this time?

What circumstances produce your most creative thoughts?

How are other people responding to you when you are being creative?

Not creative   Highly creative

1 2 3 4 5 6 7 8 9 10

Circle where you are on this scale.

What number would you like to move to on this scale?

What needs to happen for you to succeed in making this move?

Modelling someone or something that succeeds is one way to change your own maps of behaviour and will give you new ways to explore the territory.

Who do you believe exemplifies creativity and innovation?

What do they appear to do?

How are you like them?

How do you think about that person(s)?

Reframing why others 'fail' will also give you additional choices.

Who do you believe exemplifies a total lack of creativity and innovation?

What do they appear to do?

How are you like them?

How do you think about that person(s)?

Name a company that you believe exemplifies creativity and innovation.

What do they appear to do?

How are you like them?

How do you think about that company?

Name a company that you believe is not creative or innovative.

What do they appear to do?

How are you like them?

How do you think about that company?

The following is a series of situations or circumstances that we imagine you will have experienced at some time.

Take your time to consider each one, over a period of months if you wish. You are more likely to get value from the exploration of the territory that way.

In each case you are asked to consider a situation from your perspective. You might find it interesting also to consider the same situation from the perspective of the other party, or a third party. Think about how this changes the way you perceive situations.

You offer an idea in a meeting that is rubbished by someone you do not like.

What do you think?

How do you feel?

What do you do?

You watch two other people in a meeting offering and rejecting each other's opinions and ideas.

What do you think?

How do you feel?

What do you do?

Someone asks a question of you and you give the wrong answer.

What do you think?

How do you feel?

What do you do?

You watch someone else answering a question wrongly.

What do you think?

How do you feel?

What do you do?

In an exchange between two colleagues you are aware that they are misunderstanding one another.

What do you think?

How do you feel?

What do you do?

You are not sure you have understood something that is being said.

What do you think?

How do you feel?

What do you do?

You offer some information to a colleague and believe you have been misunderstood or not heard.

What do you think?

How do you feel?

What do you do?

Someone puts forward an idea and instinctively you feel it is wrong.

What do you think?

How do you feel?

What do you do?

Someone puts you down.

What do you think?

How do you feel?

What do you do?

Someone starts to describe a problem.

What do you think?

How do you feel?

What do you do?

Someone offers you an idea or opinion that you do not want and were not asked for.

What do you think?

How do you feel?

What do you do?

You offer someone an idea or opinion that was not requested.

What do you think?

How do you feel?

What do you do?

You put forward an idea and it is received with great enthusiasm.

What do you think?

How do you feel?

What do you do?

There is strong consensus in a group for an idea or solution and you do not agree with it.

What do you think?

How do you feel?

What do you do?

A group are strongly in favour of a point of view that you agree with, but one person is at odds with the rest.

What do you think?

How do you feel?

What do you do?

You feel the problem owner is not being as adventurous as they might be in exploring new ideas.

What do you think?

How do you feel?

What do you do?

You feel the ideas being generated in the group are all rather boring and have been seen before.

What do you think?

How do you feel?

What do you do?

The problem owner seems hell bent on not finding a solution.

What do you think?

How do you feel?

What do you do?

Clearly the solution has already been decided before the meeting and you are involved in a charade.

What do you think?

How do you feel?

What do you do?

You are totally confused about what is going on in a meeting, and everyone else seems very happy.

What do you think?

How do you feel?

What do you do?

It seems to be taking forever to come to an outcome that you see as obvious.

What do you think?

```
┌─────────────────────────────────────────────────┐
│                                                   │
│                                                   │
│                                                   │
│                                                   │
│                                                   │
│                                                   │
└─────────────────────────────────────────────────┘
```

How do you feel?

```
┌─────────────────────────────────────────────────┐
│                                                   │
│                                                   │
│                                                   │
│                                                   │
│                                                   │
│                                                   │
└─────────────────────────────────────────────────┘
```

What do you do?

```
┌─────────────────────────────────────────────────┐
│                                                   │
│                                                   │
│                                                   │
│                                                   │
│                                                   │
│                                                   │
└─────────────────────────────────────────────────┘
```

The climate in the group is not conducive to open-mindedness, even though that is the intention.

What do you think?

How do you feel?

What do you do?

You have now thought about many of the important issues that need to be addressed in releasing the potential for creativity and innovation from individuals and groups.

The other parts of this not-a-book give you some tools to experiment with and some suggestions for how you put these together to make innovation work.

You may be discovering that you know far more than you thought you did. If you have read the other parts first, we hope you will be able to connect your learning with actual experience.

Thank you...

to the thousands of people who have taken Synectics® to where it is today as a way of thinking about the world and **how we work together in it**.

George Prince and Bill Gordon began to make explicit a remarkable set of insights into how people get ideas and can use these to make progress in the world.

They invented Synectics® in the early 1960s. Many of our colleagues over the years have added their own experiences and all Synectics® clients build onto this process.

We have tried to put some of that learning into a format that gives you a chance to benefit from the years of experience represented by the body of knowledge that is Synectics® today.

We thank you for all your energies and trust we have done your collective experiences justice in this **'not-a-book'**.

A special thanks to Heidi Potter for wordprocessing the text and diagrams. We kept changing our minds and she didn't complain!

Jonne Ceserani
Peter Greatwood   Autumn 1995